M45

C+S

D0714821

BEATING
THE
ODDS

BEATING THE ODDS

FROM SHOCKING
CHILDHOOD ABUSE
TO THE EMBRACE OF
A LOVING FAMILY,
ONE MAN'S TRUE
STORY OF COURAGE
AND REDEMPTION

PAUL CONNOLLY
WITH IAN SHIRCORE

JOHN BLAKE

Published by John Blake Publishing Ltd,
3 Bramber Court, 2 Bramber Road,
London W14 9PB, England

www.johnblakepublishing.co.uk

www.facebook.com/Johnblakepub 🛅
twitter.com/johnblakepub 🔁

This edition published in 2014

ISBN: 978 1 78219 983 0

British Library Cataloguing-in-Publication Data:

A catalogue record for this book is available from the British Library.

Design by www.envydesign.co.uk

Printed and bound in Great Britain by CPI Group (UK) Ltd

1 3 5 7 9 10 8 6 4 2

Papers used by John Blake Publishing are natural, recyclable products
made from wood grown in sustainable forests. The manufacturing processes
conform to the environmental regulations of the country of origin.

Every attempt has been made to contact the relevant copyright-holders,
but some were unobtainable. We would be grateful if the appropriate people
could contact us.

CONTENTS

FOREWORD

I remember the morning in 2012 when I opened Paul Connolly's first book, *Against All Odds*. Straight away, I knew that our paths must cross.

Throughout my career in prisons and charities, I have seen how two particular factors can stunt a person's chances in life. One is illiteracy, which does terrible things to a young person's self-confidence, as well as making school and jobs very difficult. It's no coincidence that nearly half (48 per cent) of the young people arrested in the 2011 London riots had left school unable to read properly. The other is the lack of positive role models to help children build up their self-esteem and ambitions. Often that is down to bad experiences of the care system. Only one person in fifty in the UK ever sees the inside of a prison cell, but four out of ten prisoners under the age of twenty-one have been in care as children.

Levelling the playing field is my passion. My first career,

in HM Prison Service, was all about helping people change for the better and avoid re-offending. I started out at HMP The Verne, in Portland, Dorset, and ended up with national responsibility for training and support of staff involved in delivering treatment. So I've worked with thousands of people in prison whose lives have been extremely difficult, many of them brought up in care and many of them illiterate.

Experience and opportunity obviously help shape who we are, but I don't believe our background sets our character and behaviour or forever decides our destiny. Paul's story shows it doesn't always have to be like that. But there is a well-trodden path from the care home to the prison, and the fact Paul has never travelled that path is testament to his drive and determination to build a life for himself.

We all know that nagging voice of doubt at our shoulder that tells us we are not good enough. Imagine what that inner voice tells you when your parents abandon you and other adults take delight in reinforcing your negative thoughts about yourself. If you add in the huge problem of not being able to read or write, life becomes an uphill struggle that would daunt the most determined mountaineer.

I believe those early negative voices can become self-fulfilling prophecies, defining people for the rest of their lives. So, after sixteen years in the prisons, I decided I wanted to try and help youngsters before their lives went off-track – or to help them change, if that had already happened. I became Director for South West of England for the Prince of Wales's charity, The Prince's Trust, which helps young people develop the skills and confidence to succeed.

Many of the young people I met during my four years there were brought up in care or without adult role models and had ended up in prison. Many also lacked the basic skills of reading and writing. The Prince's Trust does an amazing job of changing young lives, but when I had the chance to become CEO of Beanstalk (formerly Volunteer Reading Help), I knew I had to take it. Beanstalk gives one-to-one reading support to primary school children who are not learning to read properly and I was excited to get this chance to tackle the problem at an early stage.

Beanstalk has a national network of trained volunteers. As well as helping with reading, these people are often the only positive adult role models children spend time with. Twice-weekly sessions with a reading helper slowly builds confidence and ambitions, as well as their reading skills. Paul has told me what a difference it would have made if he'd had a trusted adult to help him. For the children of the St Leonard's home, this kind of support was not available though, and Paul still couldn't read at the age of twenty-five.

As I read *Against All Odds*, I was inspired by Paul's journey and horrified by what he had endured. It was a brave book and a story that needed to be told, because, despite everything that happened to him, and some of the things he did as a result, Paul has shown great courage and resilience. He's an inspiration to many people who suffered in their own early years and I couldn't wait to recruit him as an ambassador for Beanstalk, to inspire children with new challenges and help them realise the possibilities in their lives.

Paul's childhood was tough and he has come a long

way to discover his real self and give his life real meaning. The work he does now changes people's lives, mentally and physically, by helping them set and achieve undreamed-of goals. He is living proof that your past does not have to define your future. Through his work and his personality, he continues to inspire people every day. I know that *Beating the Odds* will inspire you, too, though its new revelations about the appalling abuse at St Leonard's are highly disturbing.

Paul's struggles with the ghosts of his past, the memories of his childhood and the curse of illiteracy make fascinating, sometimes painful, reading. Yet, as he says at the end of the book, it's all good. His eyewitness evidence has made him incredibly useful to me and Beanstalk in our literacy campaigns, to Lord Listowel in his fight to improve the lot of children leaving care homes, and to people like the staff at Ramsden Hall school, where he works with troubled and neglected kids.

Beating the Odds is not for the squeamish. And it's certainly not a book for children. But what I want is for all the children in this country to become easy, confident readers and one day, at the right age, to be able to read this story and find their own inspiration in it.

Right now, though, I'd like everyone who reads *Beating the Odds* to recognise that we have a real chance, through Beanstalk and other organisations like it, to make sure no child grows up without that essential ability to read. It's time we put an end to this issue, and everyone can play a part. If you would like to know how you can help, please visit *www.beanstalkcharity.org.uk*.

Sue Porto

CHAPTER 1

THE BLIND BEGGAR

It was an ordinary lunchtime in the bar of the Blind Beggar. You may have heard of it. This was the pub in Whitechapel, just a mile east from the banks and finance houses of the City of London, where the notorious 1960s gangster, Ronnie Kray, coolly gunned down an underworld rival. He did it in front of dozens of witnesses. When they were questioned, every single one of them swore blind they had seen nothing.

Now I was in the Blind Beggar, my gun stuck in the back of my belt. And the man I was there to kill was standing, laughing, by the bar.

Prescott. That smug, oily bastard. Prescott had been the boss of St Leonard's, the children's home in Hornchurch, Essex, just east of London, where I had spent the worst years of my life. When the case came up at the Old Bailey, twenty or thirty years too late, he'd been sentenced to two years for indecently assaulting four boys at the home. But

I knew this was just the tip of the iceberg. Alan Prescott had presided over ten years of violence, rape and mental, physical and sexual abuse that had ruined the lives of any number of children in a home that for all of us had been a living hell. Many of them, I knew now, had come out so damaged that they were already dead. Several had been killed by heroin. One had gone off the clifftop at Beachy Head. Another, the best of them all, had thrown himself in front of a train. And here was Prescott, released straight after the trial because of the time he'd already served on remand, laughing and enjoying a beer in the Blind Beggar.

He was with a friend I recognised, another of the staff from the home. The case against Haydn Davies collapsed when the police announced that they had lost essential video evidence from witness interviews. He'd been charged with assaulting boys at St Leonard's, and had a previous conviction in 1981 for buggery. Now the two of them, Prescott and Davies, were just a few feet away, across the bar. I knew what I had to do. If the law wasn't going to give these bastards the kind of sentence they deserved, then I was. I had come to get Prescott, but I could spare a bullet for Davies.

On behalf of my best friend from those days, Liam, who never recovered from what St Leonard's did to him. On behalf of the other dead souls. On behalf of all the hundreds of kids who did survive, but could never shake off the legacy of the cruelty and the sexual abuse and lead normal, happy lives. And yes, on behalf of myself, in revenge for my childhood being stolen and my life being warped. On behalf of all those who could not defend themselves then or avenge themselves now, I would do it. I had come there to kill.

I stood in the shadows at the far side of the bar room, watching and waiting. When they left the pub, I would follow and shoot them down – a single bullet each, neat, tidy and purposeful. At that moment, I felt no rage or hatred. Something had to be done and I had to do it. I was cold. I was the executor, and the executioner.

I glanced across to one side and scanned the faces of the other customers knocking back pints at the bar. No one was interested in me, or my targets. Everyone was getting on with life as normal.

I drew the pistol out from the back of my belt, held it low down by my thigh and slipped the safety catch. There was no point in waiting. I was never going to get away with the shooting. They'd catch me sooner or later, so I might as well do it right here and now, in the bar.

And then I saw her. A middle-aged woman, ordinary as could be, sitting alone at a corner table, quietly drinking her lunchtime lager. Simple, grey dress, hair brushed back from her face. Nothing remarkable about her at all, except the way she looked at me. Very straight and level. Full on.

Had she seen the gun? What the hell was her problem? Why couldn't she mind her own fucking business?

I gave her a dirty look, but her eyes engaged mine and did not turn away. What was she doing? She must have seen the gun. I felt the weight of the squat Browning in my hand. I'd been shot myself, but I'd never shot anyone before, so I'd asked advice from a friend who knew about these things. He'd recommended this little handgun as being simple, reliable and deadly – the right tool for the job, for doing what I had to do. If this woman had seen the gun, anything might happen. She might scream a warning, she might rush me, she might faint. What would she do?

As I looked across at her, she started to cry. Gently, silently, the tears sliding slowly down her face.

'Don't do it,' she mouthed. 'Don't. Please. No.'

She shook her head slowly, hardly moving, with a look of grief I can't describe. She wasn't going to stop me, or expose me. She was just… I don't know what you'd call it. Appealing to my better nature?

Sometimes I wish I hadn't seen that. Sometimes I'm glad I did. Suddenly, I knew I couldn't go through with it. I could pull the trigger and kill those scum, but it wouldn't bring Liam or the others back. I'd be banged up for years to come, and the daily prediction the worst of the female carers, 'Auntie Coral', had made about me would have come true.

'You're rubbish,' Coral used to snarl at me whenever I crossed her path around the home. 'Look at you, you little shit. Prison fodder from the day you were born. You'll never be worth a fuck!'

A terrible curse to lay on a kid of eight or nine years old, but I'd stayed out of jail so far and I'd have hated to give that vicious slag the last laugh. I'd been stalking her, too, and I had a bullet in my gun for her. But maybe justice would have to wait. Maybe the woman across the bar was meant to be there. Maybe there were other things I should be doing with my life and my fury.

'Fuck.'

The moment was past. I pushed the gun back firmly inside my belt and walked quickly out of the pub.

4

It felt like failure then, bitter and dark. In the years since, I've changed my mind, backwards and forwards, a dozen times, but now it feels like I won a victory. Now I know it was one of those *Sliding Doors* moments, a turning point, the first day of the rest of my life. But as I made my way back home, it felt as if I had let the other St Leonard's kids down.

I'd let myself down. I'd made myself the instrument of justice and fucked it up at the last moment. I'd let the abusers get away with it.

I still had the gun, of course. I could turn round and go back. Get Prescott and Davies before heading straight for the part of Essex where I knew I could find Coral. That would mean three of the worst were dead. The fourth was William Starling – 'Uncle Bill', house father of Wallis Cottage (my home at St Leonard's), ex-lorry driver, sadist, paedophile rapist, a man of brute strength and evil cunning. But Uncle Bill was the only one of them who had copped some sort of justice.

He'd been given fourteen years in jail, so he was out of my reach. Much as I'd like to, there was nothing I could do to him there.

Still, it gave me real pleasure to think what special treats his fellow prisoners might have in store for a child-molesting nonce like him. Perhaps some of those he met inside would have little boys and girls of their own. They'd think of their own kids being threatened by a man like that and they'd find their own ways to express their hatred and disgust. Perhaps even quite forcefully. I must admit, I'd find it hard to weep for him.

But still I hadn't done what I'd set out to do, and the

blackness rolled in on me. I could kid myself about my motives for changing my mind, but wasn't it really just cowardice, lack of bollocks when the time came to stop thinking and do something? I'd been following them for more than a week, so I knew their habits and where to find them. I'd done all the preparation. I just hadn't done the deed.

I went home and felt awful. I tried to call a couple of people, just to talk about something else. No one in. I stared at the gun. I'd never really thought much about guns before. Over the years I'd had some experience with them – mainly taking them off would-be troublemakers when I was working the door at various clubs, which sometimes led to tricky situations. But I hadn't carried a gun, and I hadn't fired one in anger. I suppose, when a gun's made, it's made to do two things. Its destiny is either to scare people, which must be what most guns are used for most of the time. Or it's made to damage or kill them.

A gun that's not scaring or shooting is not really being a gun at all. It hasn't come into its own. It might as well be a spanner or a heavy-duty torch. Yet it always carries that potential within it to burst into life and become a real gun and bring pain and death. Or death without pain. A bullet through your arm would hurt like hell. But a bullet through your head? Probably no pain at all. At worst, one moment of wrenching agony, then nothing.

The gun was in my hand. There was a way out, if I chose to take it. I jammed the barrel into the roof of my mouth, shoving it so hard it scraped the palate and knocked out a front tooth that was loose. I slipped the safety and moved my finger onto the trigger. Enough. Finish.

I don't know how long I sat there, with the gun in my mouth. Long enough to notice the taste of the metal and the taste of my own blood. Long enough to think stupid thoughts. Long enough to think of my posh mate, Ian, and his comment, once before, when I'd been hovering on the brink of what seemed, at the time, like a life-or-death decision.

'You're not fucking Hamlet, Paul. You've just got to decide.'

And I sat there, thinking, not really thinking, not really deciding anything, kind of waiting for something to happen. If a sudden loud noise had made me jump, there'd have been no decision, but my finger would have tightened and my head would have been blown off. But no noise came. And no great thoughts came. I just suddenly felt very tired.

It was getting dark. I wrapped the Browning in a Tesco bag and put it on the passenger seat beside me as I drove back into town. I parked near Wapping and clambered down onto the mud and stones of the Thames foreshore. Clicking the safety catch, I hurled the gun out into the dark river and stood there, staring at the water hurrying past me with the tide up towards Tower Bridge, crying my eyes out.

I suppose, really, that meant I had made a decision. I don't think that was clear at the time. I suppose I'd decided there was something else I needed to be doing with my life, but I certainly didn't have any real idea what that was.

The original plan had seemed neat, logical and right. The abusers would be dead and I would be imprisoned for many years. I knew they'd get me for it. Even if I escaped from the scene of the shooting, I couldn't see myself holding out against the armed might of the Met and shouting 'You'll never take me alive, copper!', like they do in the old movies. Besides, if I had killed Prescott and Auntie Coral – and maybe Davies, because I could – I would actually deserve to be jailed. The same sense of justice in me that was outraged that no one but Uncle Bill was ever given a major sentence for the crimes at St Leonard's meant that I knew I'd have to pay for the revenge murders. Even rough justice doesn't come free.

CHAPTER 2

THE HOUSE
OF LORDS

It's funny how nerves can take you. I was just making
my way back from the poshest khazi I had ever seen in
my life, when I recognised the voice of my friend, Francis.

I'd known people who had been christened Francis
before, like Frank, my first employer, on the fruit and
vegetable stall in Romford Market. And Big Frankie, who
used to work on the doors, doing security. They'd have
thought you were taking the piss if you called them
Francis. This one was different, though.

This was Francis, Earl of Listowel, crossbench, non-party
peer of the realm and a leading light in the All-Party
Parliamentary Group for Children. I was just hurrying
back down the corridor into the House of Lords
banqueting room when I heard his voice ringing out loud
and clear. 'And I am delighted to introduce you today to
a friend of mine who can give you a unique insight into
the problems of illiteracy, as experienced by generations of

children growing up in local authority care. Ladies and gentlemen, Paul Connolly...'

Christ, I was on! I grabbed the cards with all my notes, checked my flies, walked up to the front and turned to face a sea of more than 300 faces. For a second, I wasn't sure I could do this. Then I opened my mouth and, luckily, the words started to flow.

I started off fairly gently, just explaining how I'd come to be in a care home and what the set-up was like – 300 or so children, living in the thirteen cottages in a late Victorian 'model village', with its own swimming pool and gym and more than eighty acres of green and pleasant gardens and parkland.

At first I tried to keep it fairly light. I even tried a few jokes, though I have to say nobody laughed.

As I got further into my talk and started to explain how far short St Leonard's was from the lofty ideals of its founders, I realised I was racing ahead of myself. I looked down at the reminder on the first card in my pack of notes.

Shit, I thought. I'd already made that point.

'Er, no. Done that,' I said, tossing the card down on the table. 'Oh, and that.' Away went the second card. 'Done that, too,' I muttered, getting rid of the third card. 'Done that. Done that. Done that.'

It was completely spontaneous, and I wasn't at all happy at getting out of step with the carefully prepared notes I'd been working on for weeks. But my audience – lords and ladies, industry bosses, politicians and media people I vaguely recognised from the telly, charity trustees, millionaire bankers and God knows who else – broke into gales of nervous laughter. They must have thought this business with the cards was some kind of comedy routine I'd worked out. Why is it that people always think I'm being funny, when I'm just being myself? I knew they weren't trying to do me down, but the whole thing was in danger of going off in completely the wrong direction.

They'd had their fun, and I needed to get my talk back on track. It was time to make it clear that what I had to tell them was shocking, obscene and something they should never forget. It was time to give them a true picture of what life at St Leonard's had been like.

I knew what I had to say next would get their serious attention. I told them how the corrupt and sordid regime that ruled our little world had run its secret empire. I told them how many of the carers just didn't care. How we were half-starved by some greedy bastards who treated the food budget as their own private bank and fed us a pitiful diet that was usually little more than bread and margarine. How we were bullied and beaten, mentally and physically, year after year. How the children of St Leonard's were ground down, humiliated and scared shitless by some of the very people who were supposed to be looking after them.

I told them about our 'house father', Bill Starling, the brutal paedophile Tower Hamlets council had seen fit to put in charge of Wallis Cottage, where I lived for nearly ten years.

I told them about Uncle Bill's raids on the dormitory, sometimes with a bunch of his friends, where he would make us all get up, strip off and stand naked in a line, while he walked up and down, swearing and kicking out at us or hitting our legs with his baseball bat. On bad days, he'd make us stand there for hours in stress positions, on one leg or with our hands behind our heads, and I still have the dark scars on my chest from where he stubbed his cigarettes out on my bare skin. I told them about Starling's taste for little boys, sometimes as young as five, and slightly older girls, which led to his fourteen-year jail sentence, thirty years later, for a long catalogue of rapes, buggery and indecent assaults.

The atmosphere in the banqueting room had changed now. You could hear a pin drop every time I paused. I heard a couple of muffled sobs, but I pressed on.

Just in case anyone had got the impression Uncle Bill was a one-off, a lone monster, acting out his horrible fantasies in secret, I told them about Alan Prescott, principal of St Leonard's. He was the man responsible for the whole place – a pillar of society, a local magistrate for twenty-four years, Labour councillor and, later on, Assistant Director of Social Services for Tower Hamlets. He was also a ruthless, leering, predatory scumbag, who was lucky to get off with a laughable two-year sentence when the law finally caught up with him in 2001.

But Prescott and Starling were by no means the only ones. This wasn't a paedophile ring of two people. This was institutionalised physical, mental and sexual abuse, carried out over decades by many of the carers at St Leonard's. Personally, I find it hard to believe that even those not directly involved in molesting small children or having sex with their teenage charges could have remained completely unaware of all this going on, regularly and routinely, year in and year out.

I don't suppose there have been many speeches like mine in the environs of the House of Lords. By the time I was getting to the end, there were a lot of tears in the audience. I felt bad about upsetting these good people, but it was clear that most of them had had no idea of what kids like me went through. They had come, I suppose, expecting a much more conventional talk about illiteracy, but they'd got rather more than they bargained for.

In the context of the rapes, the violence and the exploitation the children suffered, the illiteracy so many of us shared might have seemed a minor problem. It wasn't. Not being able to read and write was one of the factors that held us down, that kept our self-esteem at rock bottom and guaranteed we couldn't stand up for ourselves. The adult world runs on paper and bureaucracy and it will always crush those who can't join in.

There were inspections and social worker visits and record sheets and reports that should have exposed what was happening at St Leonard's over a period of nearly twenty years. But they didn't.

Of course they didn't. The files were written up by the paedophiles.

When I got to see mine, years later, after the court case, I could see exactly why none of the inspectors had been interested in asking me for my opinion about the life I lived there.

'Paul is a very small child,' one entry read. 'He is a very violent boy who is expected to continue to have problems as he grows up.'

That was probably written by William Starling, who beat me up regularly and savagely until I got a bit too

13

tough for him. Or maybe by Prescott, who would probably remember me as violent because of the way I had pulled a knife on him when I was thirteen and he came at me, drunk, and tried to force himself on me.

There was a typically spiteful comment, too, from the notorious Auntie Coral: 'Paul will be in prison by the time he's eighteen.'

When things are written down, in the right place on a form, in the right kind of words, it's easy to believe they are true.

There's a certain sick humour in looking through these historic files, now, just to see the lies the carers made up about us. I found a comment about my older brother Declan that had us both in stitches.

'Declan,' it said, 'likes wearing girls' clothes.'

I read it out to him in a solemn voice.

'No I don't,' he spluttered.

But I pretended to be shocked: 'Declan, I never knew. It must be true. It's here in black and white.'

The fact is, though, that the written word has its own power and the occasional whining complaint from some surly, inarticulate kid would never be a match for the paedophiles' files. Anyone who ever set foot in St Leonard's, if they'd had their wits about them, would have known there was something evil happening there. But the files told a different story, and that was the story everyone on the outside wanted to believe. Those words – and our inability to answer them in powerful words of our own – played an important part in keeping the lid on the cesspit that was St Leonard's.

My whole House of Lords' speech was only about

twenty-five minutes long, and I wondered whether I'd crammed too much in and gone too far off the subject of illiteracy. But something amazing had taken place in that room. As I finished talking, I became aware that the air was thick with emotion. People really were crying. But they were clapping, too, and they all stood up. I didn't know what to do and started to turn away but Lord Listowel and Sue Porto, the boss of the Beanstalk literacy charity, smiled and nudged me back in front of the audience. It took me a while to recognise what was going on. I had got through to them, the lords and millionaires, politicians and captains of industry, and they were giving me a standing ovation.

Right down at the front, though, was the person who mattered most. She was sobbing, too, and laughing, choking up and looking at me with a mixture of anguish and pride. Jo – my wife, my partner, mother of my two fantastic sons and truly the love of my life – had not heard half this stuff before.

Even when my first book, *Against All Odds*, became a surprise bestseller, topping the Kindle sales charts over the weeks around Christmas 2011, Jo had never felt able to read more than a few pages of it. We didn't meet until 2003 and I'd spared her the details of the horrors of my early life at St Leonard's, just as I'd chosen not to tell her much about the nastier side of my years working as a bouncer and a bodyguard. Jo knew the new me. In fact, Jo had helped me become the new me.

I'm not saying the old, angry, abused and frustrated Paul is gone, erased from my history. Everyone is the result of all that's happened to them, and it's all still in there somewhere. There's a part of me that's still that scared, angry little boy from St Leonard's. But my life turned a corner when I met Jo. Through her, I've become steadier, calmer, smarter, kinder. I've turned out to be a good dad, despite the total lack of decent male role models in my own childhood. I'm still not what you'd call a writer, but I'm a best-selling author, with something to say, and I've found a way to say it. The success of *Against All Odds* has given me a voice and I'd love to be able to go back now and tell that scared little boy how many people have heard his story.

That day, at the House of Lords, I had a bunch of the real movers and shakers in the land as my audience. You could smell the wealth. You could feel the power. And I had them in the palm of my hand. Jo was proud of me. *I* was proud of me. It's not a feeling I'd had all that often in the earlier part of my life. But it felt like something I could grow to like.

CHAPTER 3

RUBBISH

When I was just two weeks old, my mother threw me out with the rubbish, leaving me in the street beside the bins, near our home in Stepney, East London.

Needless to say, I can't remember it happening, but I do know what happened next, because I know that I was taken in by the nuns at a convent in Mill Hill, with their huge white winged headdresses, and looked after there until I was almost eight years old. The nuns were reasonably kind to me – some more than others – but it certainly didn't get me off to a good start in life. I'd been rejected by my own family. I had been treated like garbage.

I think there's some story about how the Ancient Greeks had the custom of putting their babies out on the hillside overnight, so that only the toughest ones survived and grew up to become warriors. I don't think my mother's motives would have been the same, but perhaps if I hadn't already got some tough little will to survive, even at two weeks old, this tale of mine might have ended before it had even properly begun.

When I come to think about it now, of course, the whole story of being put out by the bins raises a lot of questions. I know the basics are true, not least because my files recorded that I'd been in care since I was two weeks old. But did Social Services just come along, shake their heads and scoop me up, without police involvement and court cases and other consequences for my parents? Had they been through the same routine with some of the older kids, too? Was my mother a habitual dumper of babies next to bins?

So who told me about it? And when? I saw my mother for brief visits about once a year during the time I was at the convent, but I don't think she'd have been in any great hurry to give me the details. Was it some self-righteous busybody nun, telling me this tale of cruelty and rejection to help me understand my place in this world? I had a big sister and six brothers, all of them older than me, but I don't suppose they'd have known if the story was true. Anyway, I hardly saw any of them. I was growing up in the care of the Sisters of Charity of St Vincent de Paul in North London, while they were being looked after in children's homes, some of them as far away as Bedfordshire. It wasn't until I was about eight and was moved to St Leonard's, in the leafy suburb of Hornchurch, on the London/Essex border, that I first found myself spending time with any of my brothers.

My mother was a midwife by trade, so she was in the baby business. But she had presumably left me out with the rubbish because she didn't want me, any more than she wanted the rest of the babies she'd handed over for the state to raise. I'll never understand what drove her to have all those kids and give them away, but then refuse to let go.

At St Vincent's, one kind and very young nurse, Mary Littler, really liked me. She saw something special in me and eventually got it into her head that she might be able to adopt me as her own child. My mother wouldn't have it, though, and refused point blank to sign the papers that would have released me for adoption. Mary was heartbroken, but she went on to become one of the most important people in my life. We're still in touch now, and she will never really know how much she has meant to me, through all the ups and downs, over many, many years.

After *Against All Odds* came out and hit the bestseller charts, I learned that my mother was still alive and living in another part of the country, where she'd been the housekeeper to a parish priest for many years. I don't know, or care, if, as so often happens, 'housekeeper' really meant 'mistress'. But I wouldn't be surprised, because I do know that she'd never been one to shy away from doing just whatever the fuck she wanted, regardless of what anyone else thought.

My mother is an old woman now. I don't know if she ever regretted giving us all away, but I shouldn't think so. I thought of finding her address and sending her a copy of the book so she could read about how I'd managed to turn out OK, despite her best efforts. In the end I didn't, because I didn't want to dignify her place in the story. Maybe I secretly hoped someone would give her the book, though, so that she'd see how her rejected baby had told the story of the abuse she'd condemned him to.

She could so easily have approved my adoption. With one stroke of the pen, my whole life might have been different. She'd had that power and she'd refused to do it. The result had been the childhood from hell, in a children's home where bullies, sadists and paedophiles called the tune, day and night, for nearly ten years of my life. I find that hard to forgive.

The publicity around my book's success triggered all kinds of unexpected events. I did interviews for countless newspapers, magazines and radio stations and appeared live on Gabby Logan's morning TV show, where I was interviewed by an enthusiastic but rather sleepy-looking Myleene Klass. Apparently, she had started glancing through my book as preparation the night before, got caught up in it and stayed up half the night reading every last page.

'Once I started it, I had to read the whole thing, even though I needed to get up at four o'clock to do the show,' Myleene told me. 'Afterwards, I was so overwhelmed I had to go into my kids' rooms and give them a cuddle.'

Apart from the horrific stories of abuse in St Leonard's, she was particularly interested in the problems I'd had as a non-reader, before finally screwing up the courage to attend evening classes in my mid-twenties to learn to read and write. I didn't really know why Myleene was asking so much about this, until she admitted, on air, that one of her own best friends was secretly illiterate. He was in his forties, she said, and it was just 'incredible' how he managed to cope with this hidden handicap.

There was an interview, too, with Libby Purves on *Midweek* on BBC Radio 4, where one of the other guests was the Oscar-winning writer Frederic Raphael, who had done screenplays ranging from *Darling* and *Far From the Madding Crowd* in the 1960s to *Eyes Wide Shut* in 1999. We had a few minutes to talk before we went on and he told me he'd liked *Against All Odds*.

'I read your book,' he said, 'and it's an amazing story. And you know, I can sympathise with you, old boy, because my parents paid handsomely for the privilege of having me buggered senseless in boarding school.'

It wasn't that funny, really, but it was pretty unexpected and we both pissed ourselves laughing. He's the kind of 80-year-old who doesn't give a fuck about political correctness, and I liked him. Still, his comment made me realise, for the first time, that there are some very privileged people who have childhoods as nightmarish, in their own way, as mine. It's sobering to think that a lot of well-heeled, educated parents who should know better don't seem to care all that much more about their offspring than my mother did about hers.

Listening to Frederic, I realised I couldn't understand lots of the words he used. I think he must have swallowed a dictionary, as he might as well have been speaking a foreign language half the time. But he was a cheery old boy and he kept making jokes, so we got on fine, to the obvious relief of the PR minder from my publishers. I think she'd been afraid that some sort of class war would break out between us. She needn't have worried, though. Frederic and I signed each other's books, and I've still got his *Final Demands* on my shelf.

A lot of people seemed to identify really strongly with my book – and not just people who had been abused or grown up in care. I think they like the fact that I never try to make it look like I'm anything other than what I am, a totally uneducated bloke who couldn't read until he was twenty-six and still effs and blinds a lot. They like the fact that I'm someone who's struggled with my temper and my anger and come out OK in the end, despite my horrible childhood. I think a lot of people can relate to my story because, while I spent my younger years on the wrong side of the tracks, I actually came through it all to be a good dad with proper family values, a fantastic wife and two brilliant sons. And all this happened despite a chequered past that could so easily have seen me banged up in jail or pulling the trigger in the Blind Beggar and becoming a murderer.

People say that when they read my book they feel like they've sat down with me and listened to me telling my story directly. They feel they know me, as if we were friends. That makes me really happy, because that's what I was aiming for. I didn't want to write *War and Peace, Part 2*. I just wanted to tell my story in my own words, though there was an element of therapy there, too, and Jo had to put up with a lot as I bared my soul and dug back into my past.

Some of the thousands of emails I've had have been from people far away, in America or South Africa or Brazil. Often there seems to be something in my book that relates to their own experiences or seems to give them new insight into how people deal with difficult childhoods. I've had letters from psychologists and healthcare experts who've recommended it to people wanting to understand the long-term effects of deprivation and how a damaged life can be pieced back together. One psychotherapist specialising in childhood abuse wrote that she would recommend my book to her clients as 'a must-have in reclaiming power and control over their lives and giving the finger to the past'. Another email came from an eminent US psychologist, telling me that my story, which seems so very English in some ways, was just as relevant on the other side of the pond.

It turns out that as a survivor of childhood abuse, I'm a member of a large and not very exclusive worldwide club. I was half-starved, told I was worthless, punched and kicked and beaten. I had cigarettes stubbed out on my skin and had to fight off adults' indecent assaults. Yet there were other kids, just yards away, whose physical sufferings were worse than mine. And there were infants in St Leonard's who had become the perverts' playthings before they were out of nappies.

I know now that millions of kids around the world are suffering horribly all the time, and those of us who survive just have to try to muddle along as best we can. I feel pleased and humbled to think that my story might be able to help people whose experiences have mirrored mine in some way or other. And I'm proud that I've written a book that's interested academics and psychologists and psychotherapists, but also got through to less-educated folk who are just curious about how those who've experienced adversity can put it behind them.

'I'm thirty-six,' one man wrote. 'I fix crash barriers on the motorways for a living, but I cried like a baby when I read the last chapter.'

Perhaps the most extraordinary, unlikely letter I received came from Auntie Coral's niece. This poor woman had never had any idea of the terrible things her aunt and her colleagues had done to me or the other children in their care, but she had obviously read the book and been horrified.

Coral – it still drives me mad that we must, for legal reasons, disguise this evil, spiteful woman's real name – had been the worst of them all to me. She'd done more to belittle, undermine and scar me with her ten years of scorn and hatred than Starling with his brutal physical batterings or any of the others with their attempts at forced sexual contact. But no one gets jailed for what they say, even when it amounts to deliberate mental torture.

Unlike Starling or Prescott or Haydn Davies – who had actually been convicted of buggering a teenage boy in the early 1980s, while he was working at St Leonard's, though even that had not led to any proper inquiry or investigation into the situation at the home – Coral was never likely to face any sort of criminal charges. The only time she had been in danger of having to pay for her sadistic bullying was when I'd been plotting my own campaign of rough justice, the plan that came to an end when I threw the Browning pistol into the Thames.

Now, however, Auntie Coral's real-life niece was writing to me to express her sadness and to apologise. It wasn't her fault in any way, of course, but I did appreciate the unexpected and clearly heartfelt gesture. And she had a nice way with words, as she summed up her feelings about her aunt and the other carers who had betrayed the children in their trust.

'May they rot in hell,' she wrote.

And who could argue with that?

CHAPTER 4

A FUNNY SORT
OF LIFE

The outline of my life story is pretty straightforward, really. I was born into what would have been a large family, only it wasn't. My parents had a girl, followed by an unbroken run of seven boys, and I don't know why. Because every time they had a child, they gave it away to be looked after by other people.

I was born in the early 1960s, before the contraceptive pill was widely available, but I think my mother must have known where babies came from. After all, she was a midwife by profession.

I was the youngest and my mother got rid of me at the age of two weeks, so I was raised, up to the age of eight, by the nuns and staff at a convent in North London. I didn't know anything else, and though the nuns were strict, I was generally happy enough growing up there, except for the awful, empty feeling that all abandoned kids have. If you're in that sort of situation, there's always going to be a moment, round about the time you start your schooling, when you begin to realise how different other children's lives are. As I gradually became aware of families and parents and hugs and treats as things that other children had, I also became aware that they were simply not available for us convent kids.

When that first hits home, it's a shock. The more you learn about mothers, the more you realise that they are supposed to feel some sort of special bond with their children. Mine didn't. She visited me a few times, but she obviously had no interest in me. After my parents split up, my father apparently used to come and see me at the convent quite often when I was tiny. But that soon came to an end and I was left alone in the world.

The only person who seemed at all bothered whether I lived or died was someone completely unrelated to me. Mary, the nurse at the convent who tried to adopt me, was single and only twenty years old, but she really wanted the adoption to go through. My mother soon put a stop to that, though. She didn't want me, but no one else was going to have me either. She announced that she wouldn't sign the forms that would let me be adopted by Mary or anyone else, so I stayed, for the time being, at the convent.

Over the years – nearly half a century – that nurse has been just about the only constant, loving, caring figure in my life. She would take me for occasional days out, away from the convent, and spoil me with treats like horse riding and visits to her mum's home in the New Forest. Later, when she left St Vincent's, got married and moved down to the seaside, near Bournemouth, she would take me on holiday every year. For a week or two, I would be carried away to another world, a world of sunshine and sandy beaches, cream teas and buckets and spades. I'd relax into the unfamiliar warmth of a gentle, friendly family home, where Mary and her husband, Adrian – and eventually their son, Spencer – would treat me as if I really belonged.

It was the highlight of my year, and these holidays carried on right through into my dark, increasingly stroppy and aggressive adolescence. Even then, it wasn't Mary who put an end to them. The holidays stopped because I'd reached such a level of self-disgust that I no longer felt I could bear to be with these nice, loving, happy people. I stopped all contact with Mary for many years, though it was absolutely typical of her that, when I eventually got round to getting back in touch, she welcomed me with open arms and never once asked why I'd broken off the relationship.

It was a rule at the convent that kids had to move on to somewhere else as they approached the age of eight. I suppose that, even with God on their side, the nuns recognised that they were not equipped to cope with older children or the disruptive behaviour of fast-growing adolescents. So I was moved on to my next home. One day, my social worker turned up, looking very smart and formal in his dark suit, and took me on a complicated train journey which finally landed us in Hornchurch, Essex, on the edge of the countryside, a few miles to the east of London.

This was my introduction to the St Leonard's Children's Home, built in late Victorian times by enlightened workhouse reformers. They had tried to create a pleasant, safe environment for the steady flow of orphaned and abandoned youngsters who came out of the East End.

The Victorian do-gooders had picked a wonderful site and built an establishment large enough to house about 300 children, with its own school hall and church, laundry and infirmary, swimming pool and orchards. There was a bakery, originally, and craft and engineering workshops where the kids could learn a trade. Instead of one big Dickensian building, they had built separate 'cottages', each for up to thirty children, plus resident staff, in the hope of creating family-like groups. The cottages were strung out either side of a long drive that led down towards the cricket field and the farm – in fact, among ourselves, we always called St Leonard's 'The Drive'.

I've seen letters and diaries and reminiscences from several generations of children who grew up there in the early days and through into the 1960s and they generally speak fondly of St Leonard's. I imagine there were all kinds of cruelties and abuses going on at various times, but the children who came out of the home mostly seemed to feel that life there was tough, but fair. Some were even nostalgic about it in later life. I've seen a couple of letters in which elderly people refer back to their time in The Drive as the best days of their life. God help them is all I can say!

By the time I was sent there, in 1970, something had gone very wrong. The founders' good intentions had been betrayed and the home was a place where corrupt, evil and exploitative child abusers could be found, with very different ideas about how young kids should be treated. Though run by the London Borough of Tower Hamlets, the home was well outside the borough's boundaries and was hardly supervised at all. There were paedophiles and sadists who ran St Leonard's as their own personal empire and behaved as if the outside world did not exist. The only law was their own perverted and depraved lust and the children had been put there, it seemed, purely for their pleasure and gratification.

One of the survivors from my time at The Drive summed it up just recently in a comment on a social media site.

'When will this nightmare ever end?' he wrote.

Poor sod. If it's still that vivid and painful for him when he's into his fifties, I think we all know the answer. It won't.

I spent ten years in St Leonard's. By the time I arrived I was no angel and I had already got into trouble at the convent for being aggressive and temperamental. But I have to say that St Leonard's did for me what it did for hundreds of other kids. It undermined and brutalised me. It taught me that violence was an everyday fact of life, the only way discipline could be imposed or arguments could be settled. It taught me to hit and hurt. It taught me to hate and fear grown-ups and distrust anyone who tried to get close to me.

As Libby Purves put it, when she interviewed me on her Radio 4 programme, I was living in a world where there were no safe hugs. If it hadn't been for the Dagenham Boxing Club, just down the road, where they'd made me welcome from the very first time I wandered in, with Liam, as a bewildered eleven-year-old, I don't think I'd have survived at all.

Worst of all, St Leonard's taught me to dislike the person I was and believe there was nothing I could do to change that. It gave me nightmares and phobias and depression that have dogged me all my life. And I got off lightly. As I found out, many years later, a large number of the children I grew up with at St Leonard's simply never recovered from the damage they'd suffered and ended up dying of drug overdoses or taking their own lives in a variety of horrible ways.

School was a disaster. I couldn't read, so I couldn't learn. Primary school was a waste of time and secondary school was worse. The minimum school-leaving age had just been raised to sixteen, but there was no chance I would be staying that long. I spent most of my last two years at Bishop Ward School in the art room.

The art teacher was a big, ugly, Welsh ex-rugby player, with a battered nose and a prop forward's ears. He used to cane me, hard, on the front of my wrists, which hurt like fuck. But he was a realist, and he could see I had a tiny bit of talent.

'I suppose you might as well be here,' he said. 'Otherwise you'll just bugger off and we'll never see you in school at all. Just sit over there and do something, will you?'

He'd keep an eye on what I was producing and egg me on to try new ideas. There was even talk of me doing O-level Art, a couple of years early, to get at least one exam under my belt. But time ran out, well before my fifteenth birthday. One day I was in another part of the school and one of the other teachers decided to teach me a serious lesson with the cane. I was used to taking my punishment when I'd broken the rules, but there was no reason for it this time and the injustice of it really got to me. I hit the teacher, hard and accurately, with a boxer's right hook that put him on the floor and left him with blood streaming from his nose and his white shirt turning red. Later that day I was expelled, and it was no great loss to the school or me.

I was making good progress as an amateur boxer by this time, training hard and winning a lot of competitive fights. The boxing club was the one place where I was liked and respected, and a couple of the coaches saw me as a future amateur champion, perhaps even turning pro. When I left the school somebody at the club put me in touch with a friend called Frank, who had a fruit and veg stall in Romford market, and he gave me a job. I was still at The Drive, because they were supposed to keep you until you were eighteen, but it wasn't so bad if you were out at work all day. And at least my diet improved, as I was able to bring extra food back with me.

I was good on the market stall. I liked the banter with the shoppers and Frank treated me OK. So things were fairly stable for the next couple of years, until I threw the kitchen table at Auntie Coral, my evil witch of a house mother, and was finally thrown out of St Leonard's.

After leaving the home, when I was seventeen, I stayed in the same area, around Essex and the fringes of East London. I'd made a few friends down at the market, so my social life was fairly busy. I lived in a string of sordid bedsits and did roofing work on building sites most of the time. I remember one filthy bedsit where the only place I could wash was in the basin in my room, cold water only. I'd come in from working on the site, sit on the edge of my single bed, caked in dust, and eat my greasy fish and chips out of a sheet of newspaper, staring at my old Muhammad Ali poster on the wall. Ali came with me everywhere, though he was getting a bit tatty round the edges by then.

In the evenings, I'd go out with my mates, go to pubs and get into fights. That was something I was good at. I was a trained – and, by now, quite successful – amateur boxer. I was fit as a flea, small but powerful, with a chip on my shoulder and something to prove. And I was never drunk. I hardly touched alcohol – partly because I always had one eye on my boxing training regime but also because I was too much of a control freak ever to want to let go. But we didn't have to look for trouble. It would find us. We were trouble magnets. In the places we went, people would start a ruck just for the fun of it.

'Oi, you looking at my bird? Fancy her, do you?'

'No, I was just...'

'You were just fucking *what*?'

'I was just minding my own business.'

'Not looking at my girl, then?'

'No.'

'What's the matter with her? Why weren't you looking? She's a good-looking bird, ain't she?'

'Yes, she's OK.'

'What do you mean, "OK"? You fucking insulting my bird, you prick?'

'No, she's very good-looking.'

'You bastard! You *were* looking at her. Come on, prat, let's take it outside.'

People picked fights with us, and they often particularly

picked on me, as I was the smallest. Mistake. If someone had a go at me, the bigger the better – I'd beat the shit out of him. I liked to see them go down, to watch them bleed and hear them moan and grovel. I think I lacked empathy.

It was all good training for the next phase of my career, which was basically about hiring out my fighting skills to provide security for establishments or individuals. There's a lot of detail about all this in my first book, *Against All Odds*. I started doing door security work as a bouncer, at various pubs and clubs in Essex and the East End, combining that with roofing work during the day and many hours a week of serious boxing training.

As I rose through the amateur ranks, it became clear that I could potentially turn pro. I'd always had the dream, since I was in my early teens, that I could become a professional boxer. That would be a career all right. I'd make money, win respect and have all the girls fluttering round me. It wouldn't matter if I couldn't read or write – I'd employ someone to do my writing for me. And I was on course for the dream, in my early twenties, when I fell off a roof and almost killed myself.

The accident was horrific, but the aftermath was even worse. My right arm had almost been severed as I fell through a glass door. I'd lost shoulder muscles and, worst of all, I'd badly damaged my right hand and lost a finger. Whatever else I was going to do with my life, professional boxing was out.

That meant if I wanted anything more than the dumbest dead-end jobs, I was going to have to learn to read and write. I went through the humiliating and difficult process of taking adult literacy classes at night school and found that I was able to study properly for the new career I had my eye on – as a fitness trainer and gym instructor.

So I gradually started to get my life going. I passed the exams and got the certification I needed and began working, first as an ordinary gym instructor, and then as one of London's first one-to-one personal trainers. Clients sometimes looked at me a bit oddly, as I was still doing door security and I would occasionally come in on a Monday with some nasty cuts and bruises to show for a hard weekend's work. But business was good. After a few years, I found myself training some big-name clients and working on a top supermodel's best-selling fitness video, and that led to a lot of TV appearances and press interviews.

In the late 1980s, I launched my own Boxerobics training system, combining boxing exercises with more conventional health club routines in a way that hadn't been done before. It caught on, got me on the telly a fair bit and grew quickly, making me more money than I'd ever seen before. But I still kept my hand in and made a bit more on the side with security work. And eventually the day came when I was in the wrong place at the wrong time.

I found myself in a vicious, no-holds-barred fight with five very unpleasant blokes outside the club where I was working. At one point I was on the ground and in real danger of never getting up again, but it ended with three of the bastards running away and me seriously bashing up the other two.

I was charged with grievous bodily harm and the heavier charge of GBH with intent, which can carry a five- or six-year prison sentence. I had a dreadful eighteen months in limbo while I waited for the case to come to court and the trial lasted a full week before the jury, after just one hour's deliberation, acquitted me on the grounds that I had only used 'reasonable force'.

It was a year or so after this that two policewomen knocked on the door and broke the news to me that they were mounting a big investigation, Operation Mapperton, into the abuse at St Leonard's. They told me that Liam had killed himself and that only two of us, now aged thirty-five, from my dormitory in Wallis Cottage were still alive. I knew about me. It turned out the other survivor was tucked away as a guest of Her Majesty, serving a long sentence for armed robbery. That wasn't surprising. I remembered him and I'm pretty sure he was the one who was nicked in his twenties when he held up a local bookmaker's shop and tried to use a pre-booked minicab as his getaway vehicle.

So I made my statement and gave my evidence about what I'd seen and experienced over the years at St Leonard's, and so did hundreds of others. In the end, Operation Mapperton took evidence from well over 300 people. Yet, by the time the case was brought to trial at the Old Bailey, in 2001, it was stated that 'video and other evidence' had been lost.

One of the three defendants, Haydn Davies, was acquitted on twelve charges (after originally facing thirty-seven) on the grounds that, without the missing evidence, he could not face a fair trial. The principal of the home during my time, Alan Prescott, confessed to a small number of charges and received a two-year jail sentence. Bill Starling, 'Uncle Bill', the house father in my cottage, was jailed for fourteen years for offences of rape, buggery and indecent assault against eleven victims, all boys and girls aged between five and fourteen.

I was furious. This wasn't justice. This was a sick joke. Just one substantial prison sentence, after all the pain and damage they'd caused.

The trial had hardly scratched the surface of the abuse. Afterwards, the detective in charge of the investigation told the newspapers he thought there could have been seventy individual victims. My guess is that there were many, many more than that. And that's only the sexual abuse. No one was even talking about punishing anyone for the physical and emotional violence our carers had meted out to hundreds of children.

The sense of a great injustice hung over me, giving me physical pain, until, in the end, I made up my mind that I would have to do something about it. That was when, for the first time in my life, I got hold of a gun and began stalking Prescott and Auntie Coral. In the bar of the Blind Beggar, in Whitechapel, I'd come within seconds of pulling the trigger and shooting Prescott and Davies in cold blood.

★ ★ ★

I was trying to get back to concentrating on expanding my training business when I met Jo and my life changed again. This time I saw a real opportunity to build a better future, with someone who could help me grow into the person I wanted to be – settled, loved, successful, and normal.

The last thirteen years have been about trying to make that dream of a better future come true. Jo and I have the perfect relationship – perfectly loving, perfectly supportive, and perfectly capable of coping with the major dust-ups that occur when she's right and I won't back down. We have two of the best, most interesting and totally exceptional sons in the world, or so our nine-year-old, Harley, tells us. And I have had the extraordinary experience of seeing *Against All Odds* reach half a million people and draw a lot of attention to places like St Leonard's and problems such as child abuse, illiteracy and the piss-poor support kids get when they finally leave the care system.

There have been some downs, too. I almost died of infective endocarditis a few years ago and I've been left with damage and a leaky heart valve that the specialist says is going to need some serious surgery in the next few years. We'll see about that. I've got a body that's criss-crossed with scars and there are still plenty of mental scars – hang-ups and tensions left over from my past – that I have to work my way through.

But I'm busy and happy. The personal training business is going well and I've been achieving some great successes with my rehab work, especially helping kids and young adults suffering from scoliosis, or curvature of the spine. And I've been finding time to work with campaigners like Lord Listowel and the Beanstalk reading charity to raise funds and publicise their work with today's least privileged children.

When I think back to the scrawny, lonely little boy I was, and the ruthless beatings I took at the hands of Uncle

Bill, it seems hard to imagine my life would ever come right. When I think of the constant drip-drip-drip of scorn and hate I had from Auntie Coral, I can only feel grateful for Jo and the boys and the handful of close friends who've helped me get this far. Now it really is down to me to make the most of it all.

CHAPTER 5

SPEAKING UP

My big speech at the House of Lords wasn't quite my first public speaking engagement. A few months earlier I'd had an email from Sue Porto, asking me, innocently enough, if we could meet for a coffee and to talk about the problem of children who can't read.

I've since discovered that what Sue wants, Sue gets. What Sue wanted, it seemed, was for me to talk to a few people connected with her charity about my background and the difficulties of growing up unable to read or write.

So, obviously, I did.

I wanted to help Sue, but I didn't fancy it. I wasn't someone who did public speaking. I've done plenty of TV, but people don't look back at you on telly. You don't know if they're laughing at you, whereas face to face there's nowhere to hide.

I took advice first from my clever mate Ian, my go-to best friend for sage counsel and reliable words of wisdom.

'Go on,' he said. He knows about these things. 'It'll just be a few sandwiches and a bit of a chat. You'll just have to tell them about *Against All Odds* and see if you can help raise some money for the charity. It's great publicity for the book and you might be able to shift a few copies and do a bit of good at the same time.'

That's the last time I take Ian's advice, degree or no degree.

It turned out this meeting was in the City offices of a firm of solicitors, Norton Rose. Very posh. You could taste the money in the air. It was true there were only twenty people there, but I started to worry I might be out of my depth when I saw the entertainment that had been laid on for us.

With just twenty guests coming, they'd hired an angelic blonde in a long evening dress to play a big gold harp in the background while the waiters brought us a silver service luncheon. Fucking harp music! Where the hell was I?

The people at the table were all benefactors, patrons and other bigwigs. There were gilded place cards with the guests' names and titles, but the names meant nothing to me. Looking at these smooth, effortless, beautifully turned-out toffs, I was glad I'd chosen the suit rather than T-shirt and jeans that morning. I felt intimidated and suddenly started remembering little details, like the fact that I'd never done any public speaking before.

'Don't worry,' Sue whispered to me. 'Relax and enjoy your food and we'll just have a little chat afterwards. It's no big deal. You'll do brilliantly.'

I'd got halfway through the asparagus when she came back to me, slightly less relaxed.

'Sorry, Paul,' she said, 'Change of plan. Some of the guests are going to need to leave early, so you'll have to do your talk now.'

I didn't really know what I was doing. I guess I was supposed to be talking about the value of the charity's work in the light of my own background and struggles with literacy. Instead, I found myself blurting out all kinds of personal stuff about my best friend, Liam, and how we'd lost touch after we'd left St Leonard's and how I'd only found out about his suicide under the wheels of a train years after it happened. I started welling up as I spoke and I finished the talk with tears running down my face. I felt like an idiot, especially when everyone started applauding.

I was convinced I'd let Sue down, but she said I'd done well. She introduced me to a quietly-spoken American couple who told me they'd found it very moving and said they wanted to help.

I found out that the man, Jake, was the sort of US billionaire who likes to do useful things with his money. He sponsors the Chicago Opera House, it seems, and donates millions of dollars a year to various charities. I like to think that in his position I'd do the same. Maybe not the opera house, though. He was a useful man for Beanstalk to have on its side and I think he really did appreciate my talk, as he turned up again later that summer for my House of Lords speech and complimented me afterwards on how I'd put my story across to that much-bigger audience.

Generally, of course, it was much easier for me when I was talking to people afterwards, one to one. I had definitely made an impact, and Sue was already starting to make more plans. Not long after the Norton Rose talk, she told me she wanted me to meet one of Beanstalk's patrons, Lord Listowel. She hoped I wouldn't mind if she gave him my number and email address, as she already had.

The Earl of Listowel is a good man. He's a crossbencher with no party affiliations and was virtually the last hereditary peer to take his seat in the Lords. But he's no bumbling old duffer. He's younger than me, for a start, and he has a burning zeal to do something about conditions in the care system. For the last few years, he's been campaigning strongly for two big changes.

One is the upgrading of the career path for carers, so that the people who run homes like the modern equivalent of St Leonard's are smart, trained, high-status professionals, ideally properly qualified graduates, like they have in countries like Germany. When he told me about this, I couldn't help thinking about Bill Starling and Auntie Coral. Uncle Bill had been a lorry driver for Dagenite batteries in Dagenham until some careless person put him in a position to line his pockets and indulge his paedophile desires as the carer for thirty vulnerable children. Coral had been a cleaner, cleaning toilets, until she suddenly found herself in a role that suited her much better.

Lord Listowel's other main campaign is for better support for children leaving care. He has the figures at his fingertips, and he likes to point out that a quarter of the prisoners in our jails are ex-care kids – hugely out of proportion to the number in the population.

I met Lord Listowel for the first time at the Reform Club in Mayfair, not a place where I can often be found.

We had tea and tiffin, just as if the 20th century had never happened, and we got on well. He told me to call him Francis. He knew about *Against All Odds* and realised I might have a useful part to play in his campaigns.

'I've read your book and I really think you could help me out,' he said. 'I feel I understand a lot of the issues around illiteracy better now, and I'd like to get you on side with my work.'

He asked me if I would be prepared to come on board as his special adviser, as someone who has dealt with illiteracy and the problems it brings, who's had direct experience of growing up in care, and who has managed to come out the other side more or less intact.

'I'm a hereditary peer,' Francis told me. 'I work really hard to try to come up with policies that will help children in care, but I don't have any direct experience of what it feels like to have no family and to struggle with school. It's difficult for me to imagine all that, but you just know it.'

In fairness, though, he'd already shown that he was prepared to get his hands dirty by spending time working in children's homes to see for himself what they're really like. I admired him for that, and for his obvious energy and determination.

We quickly realised that this could work well. Francis has the ear of ministers, peers, big business people and individuals with the influence and resources to make good things happen. I didn't have his well-worked-out campaigning agenda, but I certainly supported the reforms and improvements he was arguing for, and I welcomed the chance to chip in with my two-shillings'-

worth. He knew how politics worked, and I understood the harsh realities of coming of age in a state care system and could talk about them from first-hand experience.

With Lord Listowel's encouragement, I wrote to the Children's Minister, Tim Loughton, and two other ministers about the importance of making sure children in care had the right sort of people around them and positive role models they could learn from.

A few weeks later, in June 2012, I was amazed to learn that Francis had given a speech in the Lords in which he mentioned me by name. He had explained my background in an abusive care home and quoted directly from my letter to the Children's Minister. I got hold of the official Parliamentary record, Hansard, and there were Lord Listowel's words in black and white:

The author Paul Connolly grew up in a children's home. When asked the secret of his success, when so many of his peers had died young, he said that he had always sought to surround himself with successful people.

For him, the route out of an abusive children's home environment was a local boxing club, and the men there who took an interest in him and encouraged him to become a boxer.

There was more, but the whole point was that my childhood experience helped personalise the campaign and make it more real and immediate.

The letters I had written were less successful. In fact I didn't get any reply at all from the Children's Minister, despite making it clear that I was writing with Lord Listowel's backing. One of the other ministers also ignored the letter and I had a fairly routine response from the third. It was a lesson in how hard it is to get a reaction, though people have since told me that one out of three isn't bad.

Since then, Francis and I have continued to nudge and prod at the Government and other bodies to keep the momentum going. We get together every now and again and talk on the phone every month or so, and he was even planning to write the foreword for this book until Sue Porto saw how busy he was and stepped in to take over.

Sue has this special quality of being a human whirlwind. She gets through twice as much as anyone else on the planet and always seems to have time to take on one more thing. If you want something done, they say, ask a busy woman. She also has the most phenomenal personal network.

She held high-ranking posts in the prison service for sixteen years and worked with Prince Charles for four years as director of the Prince's Trust, South West England. So her contacts reach right to the very top, from police chiefs, civil servants, educationalists and politicians to the heir to the throne himself. At Beanstalk, she oversees a huge team of over 2,000 trained volunteers, who give up their time to go into primary schools and institutions to provide one-to-one help and mentoring for children who are falling behind with their reading.

Sue knows where the levers of power are, and she knows how to tweak them. As soon as she saw the impact of my first, stumbling, emotional talk at the Norton Rose office, she started setting up the literacy awareness event that eventually saw me speaking at the House of Lords.

My wife, Jo, hadn't been at the first meeting, so she only had my version of it to go on – and I suppose that had probably centred mainly on my failure to control my emotions. She was certainly surprised when my invitation to speak at the Houses of Parliament came through.

'Are you sure they've got the right bloke?' she said when I told her. 'You can't speak at the House of Lords. You'll be effing and blinding and they won't know what's hit them. You'd better get some elocution lessons before we let you loose in there.'

To be honest, though, in that context, I had gimmick value.

My accent and my background – my 'realness', I suppose – meant my speech was probably a big contrast to the carefully planned, spin-doctored stuff they hear all the time in politics and business.

I know how it works. On one level, I can be helpful to these important causes because I'm not what these people are used to. I am Exhibit A. I am the tamed nightmare that gives audiences just a glimpse of the horrors they never get to see. I'm their bit of rough. And if I can be helpful that way, and help to get reforms made, I'm very happy for good people like Sue and Francis to use me when the time is right for shock tactics.

CHAPTER 6

AUNTIES AND UNCLES

After I left St Leonard's, I tried to put it out of my mind. I didn't want to keep in touch with the kids I'd known there. Not even Liam. I wanted to put it all behind me. I had this vague feeling that if I could let it all just slide away into the past, I could begin to live my own life my own way.

If you'd asked me who it was that I least wanted to see again from my years in the home, I'd have picked Auntie Coral. She never beat me up, like Uncle Bill did. And she never came on to me and tried to seduce me, like the disgusting Alan Prescott did. But she just chipped and gouged away at my self-confidence and sense of worth non-stop, day after day, week after week, year after year, as if her only mission in life was to undermine me and crush me underfoot.

I'll never know quite why it mattered so much to her

to put me down, but her constant attacks started from the moment I walked through the door.

When I arrived, as a frightened kid of almost eight, brought from St Vincent's Convent in Mill Hill and dumped in this big, strange children's home in Hornchurch, Essex, I knew nobody there. I'd been told my brother Declan was already at St Leonard's, but I didn't know him, any more than I knew most of my parents' other children. I'd never even met half of them. A brother would be nice, I thought. Maybe us brothers would be friends.

But that first night, alone in a big, strange building, with thirty kids I'd never set eyes on before, I was lonely and scared. And I did what lonely, scared, unhappy nearly-eight-year-olds sometimes do.

I peed in the bed. It wasn't deliberate, and I lay there in the dark, uncomfortable and desperately embarrassed, until the smell reached the kids near me and someone shouted, 'Some baby's wet the bed! Who's done that? Ugh, that's horrible. Who's peed in the bed, then?'

'It's you, isn't it, What's-your-name? Little Paul. It's you.'

And on and on, till the door opened and the woman I'd been told to call Auntie Coral came storming in.

'Up!' she said, 'Get up, you little fuck! How dare you do that?'

I got out of bed and stood there, wishing the ground would swallow me up.

'Don't just fucking stand there,' said Coral. 'Take those sheets off the bed and come with me.'

In the big, tiled Victorian bathroom, she turned the cold tap on full blast and poured half a bottle of bleach into the bath.

'Sheets in there. Now you. You get in there, too. I'll teach you to wet the bed.'

The water was freezing, painfully cold. The bleach stank and Auntie Coral picked up a big, old-fashioned scrubbing brush. For the next five minutes she scrubbed and scoured my arms, legs and body until the skin was raw and scratched and almost bleeding. It seemed to go on for ever.

'You're rubbish, you little fucker. Stay still, will you?'

She was furious, and her anger seemed to be stoked up again every time she looked at me.

'Connolly, are you? Prison fodder from the day you were born. You'll never be worth a fuck to anyone.'

I never really found out what made Coral hate me so much, but she was a strange woman. Looking back, I realise that she was quite young then, only in her early thirties. She was probably quite attractive, too, if you liked that sort of thing – skin-tight jeans, shoulder-length hair and all the bits. It turned out later that my middle brother, Peter, the next one up from Declan, had been one of several older boys who had been shagging Coral from time to time, in an offhand, recreational sort of way.

Some of the more handsome and adventurous boys occasionally got the call from certain female care workers to come and give them one – and few of them turned the chance down. It seemed like a victory, I expect, and anyway the philosophical view was 'A fuck's a fuck.' Peter actually claimed that Coral had been a good lay, but I doubt if her dodgy past relationship with my much older brother had anything to do with the immediate dislike she took to me.

Altogether, it turned out that four of the Connolly brothers had passed through St Leonard's before me, at various times. Maybe that was why it all started for me – just the fact that she'd seen I was another Connolly and assumed I'd be trouble.

As it happens, of course, she was right. But there was no way she could have known that when I'd only just arrived. Whatever the reason, though, she started the constant rain of abuse that night, and kept it going right up to the time I left, nearly ten years later.

All the female carers – I do find that word funny, even after all these years – were known as 'Auntie This' or 'Auntie That'. Many of them should certainly not have been employed to look after kids, and some of them seemed to be closely involved in the sexual and physical abuse of the children in their care.

In another cottage near us, the house mother was known as a harsh disciplinarian. If she heard a girl talking in the dormitory, she'd make her get up and stand outside in the corridor. Not just for an hour or two, but all night long. That's more than just discipline, if you ask me. That's an abuse of power.

Auntie Coral, of course, knew all about abusing power. She enjoyed throwing her weight around and letting all the kids know who was boss, but she did quite definitely single me out for special treatment, right from that first night.

There was another Auntie who appeared in our cottage from time to time who was even more obviously weird than Coral. She'd raid the boys' room just as we were waking up in the morning, warm and stiff, and yell at us

50

to get up and stand by our beds, so that she could see who had the biggest prick in the dorm.

'Out of bed, lads,' she'd shout. 'I want to see some skin! Don't be shy now. Let me see your willies.'

I remember Liam's brother, Seamus, telling me about another Auntie who would certainly have been prosecuted if she hadn't died before the police started taking an interest. She used to fondle the genitals of the youngest boys and girls while putting them on the potty. Later, when Seamus was brutally raped by a male social worker at the age of nine, this house mother calmly washed out the boy's bloodstained underpants and said nothing.

These people, we need to remember, were all recruited and employed to look after us underprivileged kids by the London Borough of Tower Hamlets. Uncle Bill Starling, Principal Alan Prescott, Haydn Davies, Auntie Coral and the other anonymous abusers – they were all on the Tower Hamlets payroll.

Their bosses were fifteen miles away, though, and obviously had little interest in or idea about what was going on out in Essex. When Haydn Davies was convicted of buggering a teenage boy and sentenced to eighteen months' imprisonment, way back in 1981, that wasn't enough to trigger an investigation. Davies had even been able to go back to work for Tower Hamlets again when he was released from prison. Oversight was not in fashion in those days. Nobody was watching – or, if they were, they didn't want to know. So St Leonard's was like a private kingdom. And the king was Alan Prescott, who was up to his fat neck in the abuse and corruption.

The last time I saw Prescott for two decades was a

couple of years after I had left the home. I had been nicked for what seemed to me at the time like a string of fairly minor motoring offences. I'd been driving around in my old Mark 3 Cortina, untaxed, uninsured and no licence, and eventually I was stopped. It wasn't the first time, or the second, so I knew they were going to throw the book at me.

When I came up for trial at Havering Magistrates Court, I looked up and saw the chairman of the magistrates was Prescott. I shuddered. The case took its course and they hammered me, as expected. The ban was inevitable, but the fine was enormous. Next thing I knew, a handwritten note was being passed across to me.

I could still hardly read a word at that stage, but I managed to make out what it said. It was just eight words.

'Don't worry – we'll take care of your fine.'

It was from Prescott. He'd known who I was, right from the start. It was maybe two years since I'd left the home and I'm sure when he saw me face to face he thought I knew more than I did about the paedophile abuse at St Leonard's and how involved in it he was. Anyway, it was obviously hush money, to shut me up. And I suppose it worked. I'd had no idea how I was going to pay the fine, and now I didn't have to.

I knew Prescott was a vicious bastard and a bully. I knew he'd made a drunken lunge at me once when I was doing some ironing, and I'd been so disgusted he'd nearly got the hot iron full in the face. In fact, I'd pulled a knife on him and threatened to cut his fucking balls off. The incident had ended with me hacking away at a door with the knife while he struggled desperately to hold it closed from the other side, to keep me out and keep his bollocks intact. I knew there had been a lot of talk about him and some of the older boys, but I felt sick when I finally found out, in the 1990s, just how bad it had been.

I loathed him then, like I loathe him now, but I didn't know quite how evil he was. Maybe I should have gone ahead and killed him later when I had him in my sights in the Blind Beggar. On bad days, I still don't really know if I got that one right.

CHAPTER 7

NICKING

Our main hobby, when I was in the home, was bunking off school. We didn't get anything out of being there at the best of times, so it felt like prison. Sometimes it was, too. I can remember plenty of days when all of us bottom-stream no-hopers were just locked in the classroom, without a teacher, until the bell went for break, when someone would come along and turn the key in the door and let us out. No one wanted to know what went on while the door was shut.

So we put a lot of energy and ingenuity, when necessary, into skiving. We'd go back home, slipping in through the side door and trying to make very sure the staff didn't see us. Sometimes they did, or, worse still, they'd be lying in wait for us. That was what happened the day I got my broken ribs.

I'd got away OK and come back to Wallis Cottage. There didn't seem to be anyone around as I got to the house, but as I stepped in I felt somebody grab my hair and yank at it. Uncle Bill had been hiding behind the door, and he was ready for me.

'You, eh? I'll teach you to bunk off. Get up there, you little bastard.'

He punched me and shoved me up the stairs, kicking me up one stair after another till we got to the landing, two floors up.

'You little fuck. I'll show you who's boss around here.'

I was tough, but Starling was strong, and a lot bigger than me. He picked me up, held me over the edge of the landing and let me drop. It was a long way down, and I hit the floor with a thump, breaking two ribs.

The result of this encounter was a lot of pain and bruising, tight strapping around the ribs so they could heal and over a week in the St Leonard's sick bay. It was worth it. For as long as I was sick, I didn't have to take the daily punishment of living in Uncle Bill's empire. And I got to be off school as well – all totally legit. What seems strange to me now, though, is that no one, at the school or anywhere else, seemed to be bothered too much about how I had got my injuries. I expect Bill Starling had to put in some sort of report, which would have been checked and signed off by Prescott, but that would hardly have been likely to tell the truth.

On the few occasions when anyone had spotted I was battered or bruised and started to ask questions, either Uncle Bill or Auntie Coral would get down the daybook, look at the previous day's entry and shake their heads sadly.

'Ah, yes. Troubled child. Violent tantrums. Throwing himself at the wall again. To tell the truth, we are barely managing to contain him.'

When skiving off school went smoothly, and we had some time to ourselves, we'd indulge in our favourite leisure activities – riding and nicking. Riding was a pleasure I shared with my best mate, Liam, a great kid and the friend who made my childhood bearable. Liam would come across from Myrtle Cottage, opposite Wallis, and we'd go down to The Chase, the scrubby field nearby, where all the old horses on their way to the knacker's yard were kept until their time came. We'd scramble up on top of the poor clapped-out beasts and fall off again, over and over, until we finally mastered the art of riding bareback, without reins or stirrups. Then we were off – Hi ho, Silver! – shambling across the Essex prairies on our half-lame steeds until we came down to earth again with a bump.

Nicking was a different sort of sport, though it also required us to develop particular skills and techniques. We shoplifted for fun, for clothes occasionally, sometimes for cigarettes, but mostly for food. One day, the two of us singled out a nearby shop as our target. I don't know what we were after – probably just some chocolate or biscuits to help with the gnawing hunger we felt every day of our lives. Being small, we decided to crawl in on our hands and knees past the counter to help ourselves. But this particular shopkeeper was a bit more alert than most of the others. We were just getting stuck in when he pounced, barring the way to the door. We picked up whatever was to hand – packets of biscuits, bags of flour and cans of Coke – and flung them at him as we scooted past and dashed out, laughing, into the street.

We ran like fuck, of course, down the road and round the corner, then gave it a couple more minutes and stopped, panting for breath, leaning against each other and pissing ourselves with laughter.

'Did you see his face when you threw the biscuits at him?' Liam asked. 'He was so angry, I thought he was going to burst.'

But I didn't answer. I was looking over Liam's shoulder and I'd just seen something unbelievable.

'Come on,' I said. 'He's still after us. Let's go.'

Instead of giving up, like everyone does, and standing there, cursing and shaking his fist, this middle-aged Indian shopkeeper was having a go. He'd come steaming round the corner and was almost up with us before we'd got over our surprise. Liam and I had just started smoking, which we thought made us look tough and grown-up, and that had certainly taken the edge off our stamina. I promised myself I'd never smoke another fag – and it's a vow I've stuck to all these years. But the more immediate problem was getting rid of this tubby hellhound on our trail.

We took off fast and kept going, turning down side streets, this way and that, to try to lose him.

'Jesus, he's still there!' said Liam, after we'd run at least half a mile. 'He's not going to stop.'

And he didn't. We ran. He ran. We kept going – and so did Mr Patel. On and on. I'd never run so far, so fast. I bet he hadn't, either, but you had to admire him. For a shopkeeper, this guy was some athlete.

Eventually, he stopped. We saw him pull up and suddenly look crumpled, like he really was going to have a heart attack, right there in the street.

'Come on, Liam,' I said, 'This way. We'll loop round and grab a souvenir from his shop before he gets back.'

CHAPTER 8

HITTING OUT

Loads of us kids in St Leonard's were black. Not me, obviously – I was your standard pink-ish, pasty Irish. But lots were from West Indian or African families, Nigerian, Ghanaian, all sorts. And racism was one bad thing that didn't seem to be around in our little world. We had casual, brutal violence, indecent assaults, horrible bullying and relentless mental cruelty, under-age sex and all kinds of inappropriate relationships between some of the adult staff and the boys and girls who were in their power. But the community as a whole was remarkably unaware of colour.

I think I was about fourteen when I suddenly realised that was not how it was outside. Casual, nasty racism was taken for granted back then and the big favourites on TV were things like *The Black & White Minstrel Show*, *Till Death Us Do Part* (with its bigoted, racist hero, Alf Garnett), *Love Thy Neighbour* and *It Ain't Half Hot, Mum*.

People would be horrified if those got re-runs now. But it took a particular incident to wake me up to what the black kids had to put up with.

A bunch of us had been hanging around in the street, in the doorway of the local undertaker's, and there were three or four old blokes near a bus stop. For a while, we hardly noticed them. When you're that age, overweight, middle-aged guys of fifty or so hardly register on your radar, unless they're wearing police uniforms. So at first we were just larking about, minding our own business.

When that got boring, my mate Maxwell – later, the only other kid from my dorm to survive past the age of thirty-five – started taking the mickey out of the fatties at the bus stop. Anyway, it turned into a bit of an altercation, and suddenly one of them pointed his finger and called out to me.

'Oi. You. What you doing with that bunch of black cunts? You don't want to be mixing with them fucking niggers.'

It was so unexpected, it took me a moment to understand what he was saying, or even that he was talking to me.

'Fuck off,' I muttered.

'Kid like you don't wanna be wasting your time with those black fuckers. Get off and get yourself some proper mates. You can do better than them.'

I looked round at the rest of my lot. I must have been naïve. Things like that obviously weren't as new to them as they were to me. The others were all African or Afro-Caribbean, but this was just coincidence and it wasn't something I'd noticed till then. They were my friends and the colour of their skin had nothing to do with it.

'Fucking shut up, or I'll make you.' I said.

'Yeah, right. You skinny little runt. It'd take more than you and this bunch of black bastard losers,' he sneered, grinning round at his fat friends.

'Leave it, Paul,' I heard. But I was not listening.

The mouthy guy must have been two, maybe even three, times my size and weight. He was right, too. I was a scrawny little kid. But I was an experienced boxer by now, used to hitting and being hit. I could take pain, and I could hand it out, as well. I knew where and how to land a big punch, but that didn't seem right in this situation. I could have dropped him, but I didn't.

So I slapped him. Once, twice, three times, across the side of his face.

It wasn't a fight. No one else got involved and it all seemed to happen very slowly. I walked up to this big, ugly fuckwit and slapped his face for being rude about my friends and picking on them for being black. And he just stood there with his mouth open, hardly moving, doing nothing to stop me.

I think he probably thought he was about to explode into action and kick this 'skinny little runt' into the middle of next week. But nothing happened. He just stood there, looking like a fool, being slapped by a fourteen-year-old, while his friends stood watching.

'Come on,' I said. 'Let's go. I've finished with this cunt.' And we all went inside and had tea.

I felt good about what I'd done for several whole minutes. But it soon wore off and I began to feel guilty about the slapping I'd given this older bigmouth. By coincidence, there was one of the decent carers on duty that day – Grant, a young bloke, in his early twenties, who was missing a hand and had a big metal hook there instead. I told him about it, and he grinned.

'He'll get over it,' he said. 'And he deserved worse than that for having a pop at our black kids. With your boxing record, he was lucky not to be spitting out teeth.'

He was right. I'd hurt the fat bastard's pride without damaging him, so justice was done. In fact, of course, by then I'd got used to hurting people quite badly – in the boxing ring – without even having anything against them. That's how you win. Liam and I had been boxing for two or three years by that time and we'd both become quite handy.

I suppose, looking back, the day the two of us first stuck our heads round the door of the Dagenham Boxing Club, instead of just wandering past on our way home from school, was one of those ordinary days that change the way your life will go. We were small, pale, scruffy kids and we were fully expecting to be told to get lost. Instead, one of the coaches looked up from taping a fighter's hands and called over to us.

'Hello. What are your names, then, lads?' he asked. 'You interested in boxing?'

Far from chucking us out, the two coaches at the club seemed pleased that we'd come in and made quite a fuss of us. They asked us what we knew about boxing, which didn't take long to answer, and then threw us each a pair of enormous gloves.

'Put those on and hit that,' said the younger man, gesturing to a bag.

So we did, and we were hooked. The club became the

centre of our world. Since school was just a matter of staying alive until it was time to go home, and home was just a matter of killing time and trying to stay clear of trouble, it was a huge change to have somewhere to go and something to do.

We couldn't have known it then, but the two coaches we met on that first afternoon would be important to us for years to come. They were both good people and well-known local boxing men. One, Alan Mayhew, had sons who became successful fighters. The other man, Lenny Wilson, was a highly rated trainer then – and he's still coaching young boxers to this day, well into his eighties.

There was always a welcome at the club. We'd walk in and people would say hi and ask how we were doing. Adults would come and watch us training, nod approvingly and pass on useful advice. They'd give us a Coke or a sandwich and kid us that we were making faster progress than we were. We felt supported, even encouraged, and it wasn't a feeling we were used to. Auntie Coral, Uncle Bill and Liam's house parents made some effort to stop us going to the club, but they couldn't be arsed to make a big thing of it, so we kept on going.

I remember my very first boxing gym show. I won. The youngest kids are only allowed to fight these very short bouts, with a referee stepping in quickly the moment either boxer is even slightly hurt or winded. But it gave me the taste for winning and I kept on doing it. Over the next couple of years, of course, it got a whole lot rougher and more punishing, but I was winning all the time and I suddenly started picking up titles and trophies.

Boxing rewards effort. You have to be tough, and ideally

bloody-minded, too, as I was. And you must be strong for your weight. I was small and definitely underweight for my age, but it's that power-to-weight ratio that counts. And, above all, you have to earn your success. There's a load of training to be done, in the ring and out of it – a lot of learning, a lot of sweaty, repetitive gym work, a lot of skipping and running and banging away at a punch bag. I loved it. I'd found something to focus on and something I was good at. I had less trouble back in St Leonard's as my boxing and my fitness improved and I also had a path forward, I knew where I was going. I was going to rise up through the amateur ranks, beating the shit out of anyone they put in front of me, until eventually the promoters would be begging me to turn pro.

Muhammad Ali was my hero. But I knew I wouldn't ever be Ali. He was a genius, a giant among men – and no amount of bodybuilding would take me anywhere near the heavyweight division. When I eventually turned pro, it was as a middleweight. I had my licence and I was ready to go, though fate ensured I never got to box for money. But as a kid, even when I was small, I could still pack one hell of a wallop for a little 'un of eight stone. A lot of people went down and didn't get up again.

CHAPTER 9

PAEDOPHILES

S ince my first book came out, I have sometimes copped a bit of criticism for referring to the St Leonard's home as having been run by a paedophile ring. After all, only three people connected with the home were ever convicted of sex crimes against children – Bill Starling, Alan Prescott and Haydn Davies. Maybe people think this doesn't add up to a ring.

But I believe they were not the only ones.

The judge at the Old Bailey said that although Starling and Prescott did not act together, each must have known what the other was doing. So whether they were an organised ring or not will probably never be clear. But what is clear to me is that they were not the only offenders. There are other people out there who were guilty of barbaric and disgusting acts of sexual cruelty who have never been brought to justice.

If that's the case, after all this time, they probably think they've got away with it for ever. Maybe this book can help turn the spotlight on them. Perhaps some evil bastard will read these words now and shudder at the thought that the net may just be starting to close in, at long last.

After all the recent revelations about Jimmy Savile, Stuart Hall and others — and about how everyone managed not to notice what they were up to for all those years — perhaps it's more likely now that old files will be reopened and old incidents investigated. I hope so, because I believe there's still a lot more to be uncovered.

I've lost count of the times people have taken me to task over the first book and had a go at me for writing about abuse that dates back to the seventies.

'Why do you have to go round digging up all this terrible stuff?' they say. 'What good does it do now? There's proper training and CRB checks and supervision these days, so it couldn't happen like that any more.'

Don't you believe it. Don't believe it for a moment. People are in denial, but it's still going on. Where do you think they've gone, the next generation of Jimmy Saviles, corrupt Catholic priests and Bill Starlings? Does anyone really believe there are not men, and some women, around today driven by the same depraved desires? It may be harder for perverts to find the opportunities to make paedophilia a full-time occupation, but all the background checks and case conferences and oversight procedures in the world won't stop them trying.

I felt sick to my stomach when the stories began to emerge about what Savile had done to all those kids over all that time. I knew that for me and many other survivors of the crimes of St Leonard's, all sorts of terrible memories and nightmares would be triggered. And the same would happen for hundreds – no, thousands – of others who had been abused as kids in children's homes, schools and families across the country.

Most of us from St Leonard's feel sadness, anger, a sense of loss and a wish for revenge. And most of us also feel a seething, frustrated fury that so little has ever been done to investigate what went on at the children's home and bring all of the criminals to justice.

Yet, even though we were the victims, we also feel shame and guilt, as if what happened was our fault, too. And, on top of that, there's another layer of guilt about not speaking out and getting the police involved earlier.

In the past I've beaten myself up and told myself it was my fault these evil people were not behind bars. For decades I had let these paedophiles, rapists and other sadistic brutes walk around free because I hadn't got the guts to tell the world about them, until I finally got round to writing *Against All Odds*.

All of us, I'm sure, had the same fear that we wouldn't be believed.

We had no proof to show. If we came up as witnesses in court, we'd be ripped apart by clever, well-paid barristers, who would claim they were only doing their duty and representing their clients as well as they could. We'd mostly got troubled histories of involvement with social services or dealings with the police – in many cases, leading to jail sentences. It seems like a stupid point, but we didn't look good, either. We wouldn't sound confident and articulate as witnesses and we certainly wouldn't have any documentary evidence for what we were saying.

The only thing we had on our side was the truth. And the same applied to the victims of Jimmy Savile. What came out of those investigations was the slow realisation, by the authorities, that if there were ten or twenty or fifty or one hundred historic victims who all told remarkably similar stories, somebody ought to seriously consider whether they might be true. Unless the abused kids had got together and cooked up a pack of lies, there were certainly questions to be asked about how they all knew that Savile did this or touched children like that.

If you get survivors of St Leonard's together in a room, you'll hear several different views of the place and its history. You'll even find some of them – usually girls, I've discovered – who had apparently stable and even enjoyable childhoods in some of the thirteen cottages that made up the home. For them, the stories of violence, mental torture and physical assault must seem like terrible, ugly fantasies – even now, even after the convictions of Starling and Prescott.

But once the police started digging, they must have pretty quickly seen the common threads. As in the Savile investigations, there were too many people telling too many similar stories for it not to be true.

I know more about what went on at St Leonard's than most people. That's partly because I was there, in the cottage ruled by Bill Starling, and partly because, after my book, many other kids from those years have got in touch with me. But I'm still finding out more all the time – and I'm still shocked by the new things I'm hearing.

I've already talked a lot about Liam Carroll, my closest friend from those days and the kid I looked up to and admired the most – the one who started boxing with me, who shared the horse-riding down on The Chase and who taught me all I knew about shoplifting. Liam was also the one who, twenty years later, felt so down and confused and haunted by his early life that he stepped off the platform in front of a train full of commuters at Mile End station and killed himself. He had been complaining of rape flashbacks for five years before his death, his family told me.

When the police first contacted me about the Operation Mapperton investigation, I'd not been in touch with any of my childhood friends from St Leonard's for many years. I'd deliberately cut myself off, even from Liam. So it had come as a complete bolt from the blue when the policewomen who arrived at my house told me that only two of the eight boys from my dormitory in Wallis Cottage were still alive. By then I was in my mid-thirties and the kids from St Leonard's had been dropping like flies.

Several had taken the road to hell with heroin. Little Mark Byrnes had taken a trip to the seaside and driven his car off Beachy Head. And Liam had gone under the train.

'He was schizophrenic, apparently,' the policewoman had said.

It is only in the past couple of years that I've found out how unbelievably awful Liam's life had been before I met him, at the age of eight. I have good reasons now to believe that he had been repeatedly sexually abused at St Leonard's as a toddler, before he could even walk or talk properly.

And no one has ever been investigated for that.

Abuse of infants is one of those things that are so vile

they are almost impossible to imagine. When the Lostprophets singer Ian Watkins was convicted of terrible crimes against babies and children in late 2013, he was sentenced to twenty-nine years in prison and police said he was possibly 'the worst sex offender ever'. The case was treated as if Watkins was uniquely evil.

Unfortunately, Ian Watkins was evil, but he wasn't unique. He just happened to be famous as well. Jimmy Savile wasn't the only middle-aged man who abused children. He just happened to be a household name. When these cases come to light, the media cannot resist treating them like unique situations.

Liam wasn't famous. Whoever he said had abused him as a toddler wasn't famous, either. But that doesn't mean the facts should not be investigated, even forty-something years on. I don't know who was involved. But there are official records of who was employed at St Leonard's at that time and those who are still alive should certainly be questioned. Perhaps their information will help.

Although I've only heard this recently, I firmly believe it's true, as my informant was a member of Liam's family. I had no idea, of course, when we were boys together. But there are bound to be other people who were around then and who know something about it.

Everything we have learned about paedophiles tells us that they don't just commit one act of depravity and then stop. They go on. They do it again. If it's true that Liam was raped as a toddler, he won't have been the only child who suffered that appalling treatment at St Leonard's in those grim years.

As far as I know, there was never any suggestion that

Starling, Prescott or Davies was interested in molesting infants. Even the shameless and sadistic Bill Starling, who was jailed for fourteen years for rapes, buggery and indecent offences against eleven children – nine girls and two boys – did not appear to have targeted any victims under the age of five. So, if Liam's claims can be proved, there must have been at least one other violent and brutal abuser at work at St Leonard's. There may not have been a paedophile ring, as such, but it was certainly a place where abusers were employed and placed in positions where they could impose themselves on large numbers of vulnerable kids.

I knew Bill Starling was violating children in my own home, Wallis Cottage, and that the same sort of thing had gone on across the road in Myrtle Cottage, where Liam lived. From what the other children told us, we all believed there was evil stuff happening in Rose Cottage, too, but no one who worked there has ever been charged.

There were many nasty stories and rumours about Milton Cottage, as well. We knew less about the other cottages and, to be honest, each house was so self-contained that nobody could ever have got the full picture. But I don't believe for one moment that none of the other carers was assaulting and abusing the children.

Let's be realistic. If abuse was taking place in two, three or four of the thirteen cottages and the man in charge, Prescott, was, as proven in court, a ruthless, aggressive paedophile, isn't it stretching belief too far to assume that others weren't involved? I believe there were probably many more of them, over the years. This was not just a case of a few bad apples. St Leonard's was rotten to the core.

The evil was everywhere, waiting to pounce. As one of the survivors told the police in his evidence, children would cower in the dormitories, just hoping they would not be singled out.

'You could smell the fear once night fell,' he said.

One thing that has surprised me after the Old Bailey convictions and the wide press and television coverage of my first book is the fact that we have heard nothing yet from the other carers from St Leonard's. If I'd been working there at the time and had been wholly ignorant about the abusers' reign of terror, I'd be very keen to tell my side of the story and clear my name. It's not too late, even now, for those who were innocent of any association with the evildoers to come out and tell us what they remember of those dark days.

Did they really know nothing? Did they never notice strange behaviour or unusually battered and distraught children? Were there no clues at all as to what was going on? Didn't anyone ever try to stop the abuse or raise the alarm? Before the nightmare of St Leonard's is finally laid to rest, the world needs to know what really happened there, from as many points of view as possible.

Looking back, it's obvious now that one of the forces that kept the lid on the abuse at this council-run children's home was our English libel law. It's the same thing that helped Jimmy Savile get away with a lifetime of assaults and abuse.

If you doubt that, look at the timing of the revelations about Savile. Until he died, no one ever got round to piecing together all the complaints and allegations and recognising that there was evidence there that was too clear to ignore. The libel laws meant nobody dared to print anything that they could not prove in court – and Jimmy Savile had protected himself by building a reputation for being quick to sue about anything or nothing.

But Rule One of libel is that the dead can't sue, and the moment he'd breathed his last, hundreds of dreadful accusations came flooding out. Physical evidence is hard to get in abuse cases and many of Savile's victims had no possible way of proving what had happened to them. It would always be his word against theirs. Yet once the reports were collated and the pattern started to emerge, it was obvious to everyone that the man was a monster.

The children who survived abuse at St Leonard's were mostly, like me, battered, illiterate and confused about themselves and their place in society. They had no spokesman, and it wasn't till the mid-1990s that Liam's older brother, Seamus, finally got the police and the London Borough of Tower Hamlets to take a serious look at the history of St Leonard's.

It took six years and a major police effort involving 360 interviews for that investigation to lead to the trial at the Old Bailey. And even then, it all went off at half cock, thanks to the police losing video, witness statements and other evidence. Haydn Davies originally faced thirty-seven charges of buggery, rape and indecent assault. He was acquitted of twelve charges and the judge ordered proceedings on all the other charges to be dropped because of the lost evidence.

I didn't like that. In fact, I still think it stinks. How does such a large volume of crucial evidence become 'lost'? Was it ever found again? Was there ever an investigation into who lost it and how (or even why)? If interview evidence is lost and the police believe offences may have been committed, shouldn't they be back out there again, redoing the interviews if necessary?

Everyone seemed to wring their hands and accept that 'The police lost the evidence' meant that was the end of the story. You have to wonder why that had to be the case. Why couldn't they have re-opened the investigation and attempted to re-gather the lost evidence?

After the trial, Seamus Carroll told the *Guardian* that the children of St Leonard's were 'just like meat' to their abusers.

'There was a complete conspiracy of silence,' he explained. 'We never spoke about it to one another because of the sense of shame, the guilt, and the feeling of helplessness. The staff who weren't involved turned a blind eye and pretended not to notice.

'The few children who tried to challenge them were threatened with borstal [youth custody centre], and when I did finally tell someone, he did nothing about it, because he was involved with teenage girls at the home himself.'

That picture fits exactly with my experience. There were a certain number of out-and-out abusers. Then there were a much larger number of fellow-travellers who must have known or suspected and chosen to look the other way, perhaps, in some cases, because they themselves felt guilty about their own non-violent sexual relationships with their young charges. And finally, there were a handful of naïve or unaware staff who failed to see the signs and understand what was going on. I'd like to believe there were more in that last group, but the clues were everywhere and it would have been hard to miss them for long.

To be fair, in those days there was no protection for whistleblowers. Anyone on the staff who had spoken up without rock-hard concrete evidence would have been victimised and almost certainly sacked. The whole set-up was a paedophile's paradise and I'm sure they'd have fought hard and fought dirty to keep it that way.

After the trial was over, the detective inspector in charge of the investigation told the press that the cases mentioned in court were only the tip of the iceberg. He said there could have been as many as seventy victims.

I'm sorry, but that hard-working, well-meaning policeman must be off his fucking head! With 300 or so children at St Leonard's at any one time, over a period of more than fifteen years, that is just nonsense. I believe the real total will have been much, much higher and I live in hope that there will be another investigation. But, of course, the police can only talk to those kids who are still alive. And it's probably the kids who were most horribly abused who are most likely to have given up the struggle.

Those poor sods won't ever be able to tell anyone about what they went through.

CHAPTER 10

COMPENSATION?

'Remember that no offence is past forgiveness, and that all who have been in the Homes are part of them.' – *The Hornchurch Homes Magazine*, January 1922
[The Hornchurch Homes were later renamed St Leonard's Children's Home.]

Irony, anybody? As the full horror of the abuse at St Leonard's began to be publicly acknowledged, everyone started tut-tutting about how dreadful things had been in the bad old days. People made a lot of sad and sympathetic noises. Individuals reacted with amazement and disgust. But as far as official action was concerned, very little seemed to happen.

You'd think the police would have stepped up their attempts to discover if there were any other abusers who had not been in the dock at the Old Bailey. You'd think that the sheer embarrassment of admitting so much of the evidence that had been collected had been lost would have spurred them on to greater efforts. You'd think society would be keen to provide any support it could to the scarred victims of that reign of terror. And you'd be in for a string of disappointments.

The Old Bailey court case in 2001 generated a few headlines, though the *Guardian* was the only national paper to make much of it. The trial led to a fourteen-year sentence for Bill Starling, who was then seventy-four, and the immediate release of the care home's despicable principal, Alan Prescott, whose two-year jail sentence had already been covered by the fourteen months he had spent on remand.

But there was no great effort to right the wrongs.

No further charges were brought. Prescott, who was sixty-two by this time, was placed on the Sex Offenders' Register for ten years, but he still went back to work for his old employers, the London Borough of Tower Hamlets, and carried on towards his cosy civil servant's pension. The survivors of his regime at the home and the families of those who had since died brought a class action for compensation against the London Borough of Tower Hamlets. But the local authority's lawyers and accountants were all hard at work to make sure the council wasn't too badly hit by the payouts.

I'd like to meet the bastards who calculated the appropriate compensation amounts. Families of the damaged people, like Liam, who later committed suicide, or the others who lived in misery and died of heroin habits, got payouts of £25,000. That was what a life was worth.

Others, like me, who kept going but basically had their childhoods stolen by the abusers of St Leonard's, got less. I was awarded £16,000 – a piddling amount compared with the sums people are awarded as compensation for being called names or tripping over a paving stone. There's no question that what they did to us harmed our personalities and warped our view of the world, making it almost certain that we'd struggle to build normal lives and families.

The alternative to joining in the civil action against Tower Hamlets was to apply for compensation to the Criminal Injuries Compensation Authority. But you couldn't do both. Some of those who'd suffered at St Leonard's took this route and lived to regret it. One of the most disgusting cases I heard about involved a younger boy I knew at The Drive, Thomas Worrall.

He applied to the Criminal Injuries Compensation Authority (they call it CICA, and you couldn't get much sicker than this!) and was given just £3,000 compensation after being sexually abused for eight years. As the BBC reported in 2002, CICA explained that Tommy would normally have been entitled to £13,000, but this had been slashed by 75 per cent because he had a criminal conviction.

Poor, bemused little fucker! He'd been done for receiving stolen goods, back in 1992, a few years after leaving St Leonard's, and he'd paid for his crime with four months in prison. Ten years later, when the truth about the paedophiles and sadists who had harmed him came out, Thomas Worrall was shafted all over again, this time by the authorities.

Tommy's compensation was reduced, CICA said, because of 'his cost to society'. You couldn't make it up if you tried. The 75 per cent reduction was to compensate 'society' for the costs incurred in 'keeping him in custody and court costs'. So, balancing it all out, that meant that society's net compensation for what it had done to him was judged to be £3,000 – £1 a day for eight years of humiliation and sexual abuse.

The truth is that being brought up in a cruel, abusive, uncaring and dysfunctional environment does not make for nice people who fit easily into society. Being illiterate doesn't help. Being unused to forming normal, trusting relationships with adults doesn't help, either. Being told all the time that you're shit, worthless and heading for a life behind bars – the same old song I heard every day from Auntie Coral – is not good for your self-esteem and balance.

It's not surprising if we were angry and selfish, unstable and antisocial. How were we expected to grow up? Who were we expected to learn from? Bullied children often become bullies – and there was a lot worse than bullying going on at our children's home.

The surprise is not that most of the kids from St Leonard's found life a struggle and often got into trouble. It's that any of us came out of it in one piece or managed to put together any kind of decent life for ourselves and our families. If you're surrounded by depravity, you don't stand a chance. None of the carers was ever convicted of this, but I have heard more than one former inhabitant of St Leonard's say that toddlers were sexually abused in one of the cottages near me. And I know where that has led. There has been at least one case of a victim of that nightmare upbringing who has been convicted of sexually assaulting his own infant child.

That's disgusting, unforgivable, just about the sickest crime you can imagine. But when someone's early life leaves him with a legacy like that – even the faintest inclination to do anything so revolting, lurking in the depths of his tormented psyche – you really do have to ask whether that person can ever be called a survivor.

CHAPTER 11

CORAL

The fact is, compared with so many of the children at St Leonard's, I was lucky.

True, Bill Starling was free with his fists, liked to stub cigarettes out on my bare skin and did once hurl me head first through a window pane. I was sent off to hospital on my own, on the bus, with a blood-soaked towel round my head, and the social workers were told I'd cut myself when I slipped in the bath and broke a window. No one would have believed me if I'd told them the truth, but I still have the scar across my forehead.

And Uncle Bill did also throw me down from the landing banisters, breaking two of my ribs. But he soon decided I was not his type as far as sexual approaches were concerned. As I grew older, I was stroppy, angry and aggressive and I often had a knife or a sharpened screwdriver to hand, so there were many easier targets he could hit on. In general, too, he liked the younger boys and girls. As I was nearly eight when I arrived at Wallis Cottage, I was already a bit old for his taste.

I could cope with the physical beatings. It sounds strange, but you got used to it. The greatest damage I suffered came from the mental and psychological barrage of insults, threats and negativity I ran into from Auntie Coral, every single day of my life. I never understood why she did this or what satisfaction it gave her. And I never understood how she could get under my guard so easily, and why I couldn't shake off her poisonous words.

They say some animal predators can smell fear. I think Auntie Coral could smell my intense loneliness, my empty certainty that nobody gave a fuck if I lived or died. My mother had put me out with the bins. My father had visited me at the convent for a while but then disappeared from my life. And now I had been pitched into this bleak, warped world, where no touch could be trusted and no word could be taken at face value. I was small, unhappy and alone, and all that somehow seemed to excite her to hurt me more. Like a true psychopath, she responded to my suffering by wanting to make me suffer more. Coral always wore flip-flops and I used to dread the slapping sound as she crossed the landing and came looking for me.

'Where are you, you little cunt?' she'd shout. 'Don't try to hide from me, you nasty little Irish scumbag. I'm in charge round here and you'd better not forget it.'

I was lazy and thick, ignorant and useless. Nobody loved me or cared about me – or ever had done. I'd be in prison before I was out of my teens. All the Connolly boys were nothing more than prison fodder, and I was the worst.

It was cruel and repetitive, just the same old putdowns

and insults, day after day. She didn't vary the attack much, but the endless, tireless torrent of emotional abuse ground me down. After you've heard these things repeated a hundred times, you start to believe they might be true. You can't prove they're not. And when it goes on year after year, you lose all sense of your own real identity.

In the closed world of St Leonard's, there was no referee to appeal to, no impartial adult to stand up for the children and defend their most basic human rights.

It's true, I didn't suffer the traumas of rape and repeated sexual humiliation that left so many of our children unable ever to make normal lives for themselves. But I was traumatised. I grew up angry, mistrustful, violent and unsettled, incapable for many years of forming loving, satisfying, fulfilling relationships. My self-esteem was at zero, and even when things eventually started to go well for me, I always believed I'd manage to fuck it all up.

I've got plenty of scars I can point to, thanks to Bill Starling. But it was Auntie Coral who got under my skin and did the real damage.

Even now, I'm not like normal people. You want to know what OCD looks like? Just try me on a bad day. Simple things set me off. Just leaving a restaurant after a meal with friends is a fucking pantomime. When everyone else is halfway to the door, I'm still circling round the table, looking under the chairs, checking again and again that everything's OK and that we haven't left anything behind.

Oh, and I can't bear to sit at a table with people behind me. I've got to be at the side of the room, with my back to the wall.

I eat like a horse. You have to when you do my job as a fitness trainer, as you're burning energy non-stop, right through the working day. But when I get hungry, I turn into the Incredible Hulk. I need food. I can't wait. It's urgent, an emergency. I get anxious and desperate, and people start to move away and peer round for the exits. I've been told my pupils dilate and I look like I'm going to explode. It could be funny, but it's actually quite alarming, for me and for everyone else around.

So I have my own coping strategies. I'll pull up outside wherever we're going to eat, open the car door and get someone to run in ahead and order some food for me while I find a parking space. It hardly matters what they order, but it must be ready fast. By the time I get inside, I'm so agitated I'm close to stealing the food off other people's plates. Then mine comes, and I'm OK. Three mouthfuls later, I'm back on Planet Earth and butter wouldn't melt in my mouth.

My posh friend Ian knows what to expect. He's got class. He's Essex aristocracy. His cousin's daughter is the lovely Lucy Mecklenburgh from *TOWIE*. Ian knows what to do. He gently steers people aside to let me get at the food without harming anybody and he reassures everyone that he's in control of this rampaging idiot.

'Don't worry. He's been reading the *Daily Mail* this morning and it always gets him like that,' he tells people, helpfully.

That's the kind of thing he thinks is funny. Fuck him – if he wasn't such a loyal bloke, through thick and thin, I'd tell him where to get off. He does care, though, and he always has my best interests at heart. You can tell he's thinking ahead all the time. Even when he's wearing a smart business suit, he'll make sure he's got a bar of chocolate in his pocket, just to top me up in an emergency.

The fact is my thing with food is not just about calories. It's an emotional hang-up, too, and it's obviously another part of the legacy of St Leonard's. We were starved of proper food and we were starved of affection, support, even just acceptance. And we watched Bill Starling feed his face while we were kept permanently hungry, our empty bellies just another aspect of the slow torture of our daily lives. That pain was about neglect, as well as nutrition. As a result, food is never just food for me. It has a symbolic value that people from more normal backgrounds cannot understand.

If I come in and people are eating and I'm not offered some, I feel that pang again. It doesn't matter if I've eaten a full meal half an hour ago. It's not about being hungry. It's just that not being able to share food when others are eating makes me feel left out, excluded and victimised. It takes me back, and it really hurts.

There were times, before we'd talked it through, when Jo watched in horror as I reacted to this kind of situation. I would be shirty and aggressive, snapping at her and anyone else who was around, behaving like a bear with a hangover. She must have wondered what the hell was going on, and even worried about my sanity. Now she makes allowances and I try to keep within normal limits, but food is always a loaded subject.

Of all the bad things that happened at St Leonard's, the grinding, deliberate neglect was one of the worst. Clearly the sexual abuse of children was right at the top of the scale of depravity. But I would place the emotional abuse and wilful neglect next, in terms of the permanent damage done to who knows how many kids. Simple physical battering was something you learned to endure and recover from. But the damage to a growing child's emotional balance never seems to heal. And Auntie Coral was the expert at inflicting that kind of pain.

I'm over fifty now and I still think about Coral every day of my life. I can't put her out of my mind. I hated her for what she did to me.

She was a nightmare.

But she was *my* nightmare.

It sounds insane, but despite everything, this vicious, sadistic woman was the nearest thing I had to a parent – and there was no one else around. I suppose everyone needs some sort of approval and validation from someone and there was nowhere else to go. I hated her, but I needed something from her. She and Uncle Bill made a point of making my life a misery. But they were what I had, and they were all I had.

There must be millions of 'proper' families where the parents are brutal, unkind or uncaring and the children just grow up thinking that's what life is like. Home is home and family is family. Even in the most extreme cases, there is often some sort of bond that survives everything. I know it's a cliché in child protection circles that the most abused children often try to cover up for the abuser – the father or the uncle or the much-loved family friend – even when that person has tortured and hurt them. Perhaps the idea of being utterly alone is so completely terrifying that any contact is better than none.

If you'd asked me about all this at the time, I'd have told you to fuck off. I could only see the hate. I'd have laughed if you'd said I wanted any kind of relationship with my tormentors. I could not wait to be eighteen, so I could get out. I couldn't wait to escape St Leonard's.

When that moment arrived, you might think I'd have been delighted. I'd have thought so, too. To my surprise and horror, I was devastated... and scared stiff.

The end had come quickly. I'd brought in some food after work at the fruit and veg market and I was cooking it up in the kitchen when Auntie Coral came in and started needling me with all the usual stuff. She wouldn't stop. I was a thug. I was a lout. Worse still, I was a Connolly (I sometimes wonder just how important to her that relationship with my brother Peter had been).

I tried to let it wash over me, but this time I couldn't. Like reading, anger management was one of the things we weren't taught in that environment.

'If she doesn't just shut the fuck up...' I thought.

But she didn't. I'd had enough. There was a long wooden kitchen table between us, covered in plates and cups of tea and coffee. I grabbed it by the edge and flung it hard in her direction. It flew several feet across the room, as dishes and cups smashed to the floor. It was a big, heavy table and I don't know what I was trying to do, but I think I wanted to crush her underneath it. And I think she realised, because she started to scream – a high, piercing, infuriating shriek.

'You fucking slag,' I yelled. 'I'll rip your fucking head off!'

I was on pure adrenalin. I rushed at her and stood with

my face a couple of inches from hers, roaring at her like a wounded lion.

'I'll kill you, you bitch. I'm going to get you now.'

She stood there shaking, her mouth open and her eyes staring. She'd gone too far and now she was shitting herself. Suddenly, she was in my power. I wanted to hurt her and she knew it. I'd lost it and Coral was in real physical danger. I hadn't actually laid a finger on her, but I knew if I didn't get out, I really would kill her. I ran from the kitchen and flung myself down on my bed in the dorm, sobbing my heart out.

In the looking-glass world of Wallis Cottage, where Uncle Bill's paedophile assaults on the young girls and vicious physical attacks on me and other boys were part of the routine of life, this was classed as a violent incident that called for a visit from the police. Everyone stood around and tut-tutted, while the policemen talked to the carers and someone was sent to look for Prescott, the principal. Eventually, it was decided that I was too mad, bad and dangerous for St Leonard's and I'd have to go, even though I wasn't yet eighteen.

I should have been happy. The prison doors were open and I was free to walk out and find my own destiny. But now I desperately wanted to stay.

I suppose the idea of home is different for all of us. Home is supposed to be where your loved ones are – if you've got loved ones. It's where you can relax and be yourself. But I could never relax there, and who knows who I really was at that stage?

Maybe home is just where you're used to being.

The St Leonard's home was Paul Connolly's home. It

was the scene of so many bad things, but it was where I'd belonged since I was eight. It was where I came back to after being caned and beaten at school, and after being hit by a car – and later a bus and a motorbike – because I'd never been properly taught to look before crossing the road. It was the cave I crawled into to lick my wounds. The Home was home, and to have it taken away was shattering.

So I lost my home and I lost my substitute parents, crap though they were. And it felt as if my life had been turned upside down.

I knew next to nothing about the outside world. I'd never had things like keys. I didn't know what things cost. I didn't know anything about the ordinary mechanics of how life worked. I had two fixed points – the boxing club and my work with Frank at the market – and everything else was just up in the air.

CHAPTER 12

MUHAMMAD ALI
AND ME

In 1964, when I was still less than two years old, Muhammad Ali won the world heavyweight boxing championship. He was a 7–1 underdog when he took the title from Sonny Liston. The mouthy kid from Kentucky had been known as Cassius Clay and 'The Louisville Lip', but he celebrated by changing his name to Ali and his nickname to 'The Greatest'. And he was.

I didn't see his early fights. There were no videos then and when something on TV was gone, it was gone. Ali was stripped of his title and lost nearly four years of his career when he was banned from boxing following his refusal to fight in the Vietnam War. By the time he had fought his way back and became world champion for the second time, Liam and I had started training at the Dagenham Boxing Club. Ali was our hero. We watched the great fights with Joe Frazier and gasped at the 'Rumble in the

Jungle', when Ali knocked out George Foreman in the eighth to win the world title back.

We couldn't believe how different Ali was. He was clever, brave and fast. At fifteen stone, he was very light for a title contender, but he was the first boxer to bring real hand speed and footwork to the heavyweight division.

Ali said he'd float like a butterfly and sting like a bee, and he did. He broke every rule. He'd do his little routine, the Ali Shuffle, in the middle of the ring. He would drop his guard and dance around with his hands at waist level or dangling by his sides, leaving his head unprotected, against the best boxers in the world. It was suicidal. He was betting on his ability to move his face faster than his opponents could move their fists. You can try it at home if you like, but heads just aren't built to do that.

Against Foreman, in 1974, in Zaire for the Rumble in the Jungle, he did it all wrong again. This time he didn't float or sting for half the fight. He backed up on the ropes, covered up with his arms and let Foreman slug away at him, round after round, until he'd punched himself out and was exhausted. It looked like a recipe for disaster, but as Foreman tired, Ali was able to take him out. Foreman knew he'd been done, and I'll never forget what he said: 'Muhammad out-thought me and out-fought me.'

Ali's boxing brainpower was obvious. But he'd been 376th in a year of 391 when he left school. I reckoned that told me something. I was shit at school, too, but maybe school wasn't everything. Ali said, 'I said I was The Greatest, not The Smartest' and he'd actually been turned down for the US Army draft the first time round because he could hardly read or write. I could see parallels.

I was no Ali, but I was good. As I went through my teens, I was regularly winning fights at higher and higher levels and Tommy Butler, one of my trainers at the Dagenham club, was an England coach. He knew a good boxer when he saw one and he said he could see me making the national team.

When I left school and started work on Frankie's fruit and veg at Romford market, I kept on boxing. And when I finally left St Leonard's, just before I was eighteen, I kept the boxing going. I was a rough, tough kid, with both ring and street fighting skills. I could fight fair or fight ugly, as required, so I was starting to earn some good money in the evenings doing door work as a bouncer at a few pubs and clubs. I'd work at various different day jobs, too, but I gradually found my way into doing a lot of roofing work. I was strong, agile, willing and basically scared of nothing, I'd skip across the rooftops with a confidence that had the older guys shaking their heads.

'You be careful,' they'd say. 'One day...'

But all this was just temporary. I was on my way to my real career, as a proper professional boxer. It was what I was made for. I wasn't all that interested in money, but I was very interested in girls and they seemed to like nice things and being treated well. If I could turn professional and make it work, I'd get anything up to ten grand a fight. I'd be rolling in it, and I'd be fighting them off.

By the time I'd registered with the British Boxing Board of Control and got my licence to fight professionally, in 1986, boxing had changed. The new star was Mike Tyson, who won the world title when he was just twenty years old – the youngest ever – hammering the WBC champion, Trevor Berbick, in just two rounds. Tyson was a street kid, an animal. He was bloody terrifying. At his peak, he was unstoppable. I could see how he did it. He punched hard, moved fast, defended well and had a great trademark combination – right hook to the body, right uppercut to the chin – that dumped one challenger after another on the floor. But he was also the meanest fucker you've ever seen.

I admired Tyson as a boxer, but he didn't have the magic of Ali, who had made every title fight a huge event. Back at St Leonard's, us kids would be glued to the television, like people around the world, amazed at the unexpected tactics he'd use and his unbelievable speed of thought and hand. He had made boxing something special for everyone.

When Ali fought, you felt the referee was there to make sure there was no dodgy business going on: 'Touch gloves and may the best man win.' But when Tyson fought, the ref's main function seemed to be to make sure he stopped fighting at the end of the bout and didn't tear his victim's liver out and eat it. In his second title fight with Evander Holyfield, he famously bit off a chunk of the champion's ear.

Luckily, I was a middleweight, so however far I went, I'd never be in any danger of a meeting with Tyson. There were some frighteningly good middleweights around in my generation – Marvin Hagler, Sugar Ray Leonard and Thomas 'Hitman' Hearns, for starters – but none of them was a known cannibal.

If you don't know boxing, you may not know just how much difference there is between the amateurs and the pro game. Amateur boxing is a sport where victory is usually decided on points. Knockouts are rare, bouts are much shorter and, of course, the motivation becomes very different when you are doing it professionally. When boxing becomes business, it's a mean, hard game.

For any boxer, turning professional is a big step, as there's no going back. Even if you've fought just once as a pro, you can't ever step into the ring for an amateur bout again. That wasn't going to bother me, though. I had been dedicated to the idea of becoming a professional boxer since I was about thirteen and I'd been working to prepare myself, putting in the gym sessions and the road work, the sparring and the fights, year in and year out, to build up my strength and my skills. Now I was coming up to twenty-four and I was ready to go. Not as young as Ali or Tyson when they started, but still not old for a new pro. But fate had other plans for me.

I was working on a roof at a place in Upminster one day, using one of those ladders that's held in place by a big hook that goes over the ridge, when something went wrong. We'd been cutting corners to keep the price of the job down, so we weren't using any scaffolding.

For some reason, the hook came unhitched, the ladder began to slip and I found myself desperately scrabbling for grip on the smooth tiles as I slid slowly towards the edge of the roof. It seemed like for ever, but there was no escape. I fell off, plummeted to the ground and was only saved by the happy accident of smashing into a glass door that had been left leaning against the wall of the house. If that door hadn't been there to break my fall, I'd have been a goner.

In the silence that followed, I was amazed to realise I was still alive. I wasn't even in great pain. I'd certainly got off lightly, as falling from that height could easily have left me dead or paralysed. For a few seconds I just sat there, surrounded by broken glass. Then I took stock of the situation and got to my feet. Lucky, eh? The other guys from the site came running but for some reason I panicked and started to run away from them.

'Stop! Come back, Paul. What the fuck are you doing? Sit down, mate. You're hurt.'

I was running round like a headless chicken, like something out of a horror movie, with a fountain of blood pumping from my lacerated shoulder with every step I took.

'For fuck's sake, Paul. We're trying to help you.'

I was gradually beginning to realise something was wrong with my arm. It was hanging limp, almost severed by the glass of the door. My right hand was a mess, too. You could see inside it and see the bones. There was a lot of blood now and one of the younger lads kept throwing up whenever he looked across at me.

They put me on the ground and I sat in a warm puddle of blood as we waited for the ambulance. The arm wasn't hurting, but I felt as if I'd been punched in the back. I found out later that the glass had stabbed through and punctured my lung.

The paramedics were quick, efficient and reassuring. I was slipping in and out of consciousness as they cut the clothes off to get at my wounds. But they seemed to have a lot of work to do before they moved me, and the ambulance certainly didn't waste any time getting me to the Oldchurch Hospital in Romford. We had lights and sirens and the ambulance bumped and swayed as we shot off through the traffic.

It was just as well they were quick. By the time we got to the old hospital, I was technically dead. They got the transfusion going just in time to pull me back, but there was a lot of damage to be sorted out.

While the surgeons worked to reattach my arm and deal with the punctured lung, somebody had somehow managed to get in touch with my sister, Anne. They asked her for the OK to amputate my right hand, which was in a terrible state. The glass had effectively sliced it in half, right up the middle.

Anne refused to give permission, thank God, so they set about trying to save as much of my hand as possible. Considering the state it was in, they did a good job, too. In the end, about six months later, I lost the top two joints of my ring finger and the pinkie was permanently damaged. My hand would never get its full range of movement back and there's still a huge scar stretching from the base of my middle finger right up to the wrist, but that's very different from not having a hand at all.

As I lay there recovering, in the days that followed, I knew I was lucky to be alive. I was lucky to still have my right arm. The anterior deltoid muscle at the front of the shoulder had been destroyed, but the doctors were optimistic that my arm would eventually be restored to something like full working order. I was going to have a usable right hand. But I was not going to have the mighty right fist that would carry me to the top as a middleweight boxer.

As a career option, boxing was gone. The only goal I'd set myself, all these years, had been snatched away in a stupid, pointless accident.

In the half-light of the hospital night, listening to the snoring of the other patients and the dull hum of the machines, I hit a real low. What the fuck was left for me now? Nobody cared much. I was on my own. Maybe it would have been better if that glass door hadn't been there and I'd just been killed outright by the fall from the roof.

I had no skills that would do me any good. I couldn't even read and write. I was hurt and angry, ready to explode with rage and frustration. My dreams – launched thirteen years earlier when two small, scruffy boys wandered into Dagenham Boxing Club and nurtured as I watched Muhammad Ali's greatest fights – were sunk without a trace. What would I do now? What would Ali do? It was all right for him. He was The Greatest. I was in my twenties, but right now I felt just like the frightened little boy Auntie Coral used to pick on so relentlessly when I was at St Leonard's. I could still hear her, right there in my ear.

'You're nothing, you little fuck. Prison's the only place you're going. Who ever loved you? Nobody, that's who... and nobody ever fucking will.'

I'd stayed clear of prison so far, but that wasn't saying much. And if working as a doorman or a bodyguard on the edge of the East London underworld was my only option, I might very well get dragged into some really bad stuff.

I turned my face to the wall and tried to imagine a future for myself. Nothing. I didn't know where to begin.

Without boxing, there was no road ahead, not even a starting point. But maybe that idea of asking myself how Ali would act in my situation was as good a place as any.

What would Ali do?

It wasn't an answer, but it was a very useful question. I fell asleep smiling, thinking of how my hero had changed his tactics so completely and unexpectedly to outwit George Foreman in the Rumble in the Jungle. Maybe there was some way, after all. Maybe Ali could show me the way forward.

CHAPTER 13

HOW READING CHANGED MY WORLD

When I woke up the next day, things felt different. I was still in hospital, still in the early stages of a long recovery from some very serious injuries.

'I don't want to depress you, Paul,' one of the doctors had said, 'but it could be two years, maybe more, before you're back in decent shape.'

So it was going to take time, and I still didn't know what I was going to do as a career, now that boxing was ruled out. But I knew I'd made a breakthrough with that question about what Muhammad Ali would do. There was something in that.

One thing Ali wouldn't do is give up. I knew all his greatest lines, and he had a good one for this situation.

'Inside of a ring or out, ain't nothing wrong with going down. It's staying down that's wrong.'

The other thing Ali wouldn't do is keep on banging his head against a brick wall. If what he was doing wasn't working, he'd change tack and do something different. He'd switch tactics from one fight to the next, or from one round to the next, or even for the last thirty seconds of a round. He'd come up with a new trick or a new combination. Even when Ali was on top of the world, he was always getting better, always learning new ways to fight.

My first target was to get back to something like normal health. I made good progress, but there were some difficult decisions to be taken. As my right hand started to recover, it was clear that two fingers were never going to be right again. The little finger was stuck at an odd angle, but the worse problem was my ring finger. This was locked bent, crooked over to touch my palm. The finger couldn't move and its position meant that it got in the way whenever I tried to do anything. About six months after the accident, the doctors discussed it with me and we decided it should be amputated at the first joint, so as to leave me with a hand I could use fairly normally.

A lot of people shudder at the idea of an amputation, but the actual operation didn't bother me too much. I stayed awake and talked to the surgeon while he numbed my hand and did what we'd agreed. To tell the truth, it was interesting, rather than horrifying. They just get a scalpel and cut neatly round the joint. Then they saw away for a bit and then go snap – and that's it. They sew it up and you're done.

There was another bloke in there that day for a similar procedure and he'd got himself in a terrible state before the op, saying it was like a death, like losing a loved one. It didn't worry me like that. I knew it was supposed to give me back fairly full use of my hand and, to be fair, it's been obvious over the years that the doctors were quite right. The hand works and I'm not even aware of it most of the time.

Once I was up and about, the next priority was to get some money coming in. It was going to be a while before I could get back to doing the doors or other security work, so I had to take what I could get – mainly odd bits and pieces of building work and occasional shifts driving a minicab. I didn't need much to keep me going, but I was going to need plenty of time and energy for the big change I was about to make.

I'd decided what Ali would do. And I was going to do it. I was going to take the initiative to alter my situation by getting rid of the biggest handicap I had.

Somehow or other, I was going to learn to read and write.

* * *

You're reading this book so it's going to be hard for you to imagine for one minute what it's like not to be able to read and write.

Trust me, it's hell. Every little shit in any position of authority can run rings round you. People can tell you black's white and wave a form or any old piece of paper at you and you don't even know if they're telling the truth. You can't leave a note for a friend or make sense of instructions, or get information from a website or news from a newspaper. You can't function like everyone else.

Believe me, I know. I couldn't read or write, even at the most basic level, till I was in my mid-twenties. And if I was angry and frustrated by everything else that had happened to me during my time at St Leonard's, the fact that I came out into the world without that basic equipment was one of the worst effects of it all.

People who can't read and write feel shut off from everything around them. It marks them out as losers. And it's no coincidence that the prison system is full of people, mostly men, who have this crippling handicap. The figures show half the men in prison have worse reading and writing than an eleven-year-old and only twenty per cent could fill in any sort of job application. A quarter of those in jail have very low IQs – less than seventy. At the bottom of the barrel, five to ten per cent simply cannot read at all. That's about 8,000 people at any one time.

I wasn't in jail – though I came very close at one stage, before being cleared of charges of GBH and GBH with intent – but I felt just as imprisoned.

I can read now, and I saw a government report a couple of years ago that said there were 1.7 million people in Britain without the basic reading and writing skills you'd expect in kids of five to seven years old. Is that a civilised society? Literacy's a basic human right, but this country doesn't care enough to make sure everyone has the ability to use the written word. There are some great charities, like Sue Porto's Beanstalk and the National Literacy Trust, that are trying to help. But we shouldn't need them. This is the 21st century, for fuck's sake! No one should be leaving school without decent reading and writing skills. I'm not talking about Shakespeare, but being able to read an email or a birthday card would be a start.

By the time St Leonard's had finished with me and spat me out into the world, I could hardly do much more than write my name. There was a lot I didn't know, as well. Because I couldn't read, I only knew what I could remember and hold in my head.

I'll give you an example. I knew the days of the week, of course. Who wouldn't? But I honestly did not know the months of the year and the order they came in. Can you imagine that, in a lad of almost eighteen?

I couldn't read *The Sun*, not even the headlines. I'd walk past shops and see all the signs in the windows, but I never knew what the special offers were. I'd pretend my eyes were worse than they were.

'What's that say?' I'd ask. 'I really need to get some glasses sorted out.'

And someone, if I was lucky, would laugh and read out the words. Buses and trains were a nightmare. In a café or a pub, I'd play safe so I didn't have to come face to face with a menu – 'Oh, you choose what you like, darlin'. I'll have the same as you.' In fact, that's something I still do. And as for looking for work, I'd always be relying on word of mouth and introductions. People take advantage. People take the piss.

Sometimes you can hide it, sometimes you're rumbled. Either way, without reading, you're a second-class citizen – and you get reminded of it a hundred times a day.

Even now I break out in a cold sweat whenever there are forms to fill in, knowing that what takes other people five minutes is likely to take me twenty. If there's any choice in the matter, I take the forms home and get Jo to help me. And I've never really got the alphabet nailed down. I remember Harley reciting his alphabet when he was five and he'd first started school. He got the order of the letters wrong. I was correcting him and he was whining 'Oh, Dad, that's what they told me' when Jo's voice came drifting down from upstairs.

'Harley's right, Paul. Let him get on with it. Don't get him confused when he's learned it right.'

Since *Against All Odds* became a bestseller, loads of people have asked me whether the other kids at St Leonard's, the ones who were better at reading, ever offered to help us out and help us learn.

What other kids? As far as I know, there weren't any of us, except maybe Liam, who were able to learn to read properly. No one in the home ever encouraged us or tried to help us with reading. No one seemed to give a damn whether we learned or not. We got to believe that not being able to read or write was our natural destiny. Those things weren't for the likes of us.

We were left further and further behind the other kids as we rose up through junior school. The school was St Mary's Catholic School, Hornchurch, and I was there from the age of eight until I was eleven, without actually learning anything much at all. When the eleven-plus exams came around, I sat silently in front of the English test paper for an hour. I couldn't even read the questions, so naturally I failed. So did my mates from the home, for much the same reason.

But something odd happened. I couldn't do the reading and writing parts of the exam, of course, and I couldn't do much with the arithmetic either. But there was another test that was to do with non-verbal, non-mathematical problems – puzzles, really, involving tasks like fitting shapes together or spotting the odd one out in a line of objects.

This was more of an IQ test, I suppose. I'd never seen this kind of test before, but the answers, most of them, seemed pretty obvious to me. So I did quite well at it, and someone must have noticed. As a result, when we all moved up to start at Bishop Ward Catholic School in Dagenham, I was placed in the middle class of the year, while my mates from the home were dumped in the bottom stream.

It might have been a compliment, a sign that I had a bit of untapped brainpower behind the stroppy façade. I'd never thought I was thick, but it's hard to make comparisons if you can't read and have zero general knowledge. This objective test showed there was some potential, and I suppose someone thought that putting me up a class might stimulate me to make more of that.

But it didn't work. I suppose it might have done, if I'd somehow been able to learn to read overnight. As it was, I was stuck in the middle of a class of thirty or so eleven-year-old boys, almost all of them bigger and better-fed than me, who had all been reading for several years and thought it was hilarious that I couldn't do what their six-year-old sisters could manage. They picked on me, ruthlessly and relentlessly, every hour of the day.

As far as they were concerned, I was the perfect target – a skinny, angry and conveniently small kid from a children's home, in a cheap school uniform with a free dinner ticket. I punched a couple of them, but they kept on doing it.

The teachers decided I was trouble, but kept forgiving me and giving me second and third chances I didn't want. They seemed dead set on keeping me there, until, in the end, all I wanted was to be back down with my mates, with the rest of the losers, in the bottom class. I finally got my wish and my one excursion into the higher levels of academia was over.

Even allowing for the number of times we skived off, you might think some of the teachers would have noticed the state we were in. Bill Starling was not the only house father who liked to throw his weight around and we were often turning up in school bruised, cut and battered. We were always dressed in the cheapest, shoddiest clothes, often obviously second-hand. And we were all small, all underweight and all permanently hungry.

It seems strange now that no one on the outside asked the obvious questions about these bedraggled and underfed kids who turned up at school most days. I had blinding, migraine-type headaches time and again. No one commented on the fact that they always went away once I'd had some proper food. Didn't anyone notice that all the children from the home were smaller than the other kids of their age? Didn't they see the way we ate our food – quickly, urgently, as if we hadn't seen a meal in weeks, or as if someone might snatch it away from us?

In the context of all the brutality and paedophilia, the fact that carers like Bill Starling creamed off the home's grocery budget over many years and fed us on the bare minimum of cheap and nasty food seems almost trivial. But that was theft and that was cruelty, too.

The money that should have gone to buy nutritious

meals to build our growing bodies ended up paying for Uncle Bill's booze and fags. Most days we filled up on bread and marge, with the odd fish finger or a lump of bright pink Spam and a dollop of baked beans or tinned spaghetti. Starling would sit there right in front of us, tucking into his steak with chunky chips and his favourite Edam cheese, while we drooled with envy. It was like Oliver Twist, but anyone who said 'Please, sir, I want some more' would have been left bruised and bleeding. Uncle Bill didn't like to be interrupted while he was enjoying his dinner. There are plenty of health problems today among the survivors of St Leonard's that surely must have had their roots in our piss-poor, almost veg- and vitamin-free, diet.

To be fair, there was just one teacher at the school who showed a bit of concern. He'd clocked that something wasn't right and it obviously puzzled and bothered him. He asked me once why I was always covered in cuts and bruises, though I'm still not sure he believed me when I said it was because we were routinely beaten up by some of our carers in the home.

He was a good man, though, Mr Molloy, and he did press it further. He even made the effort to come down to St Leonard's once to try to see for himself what was going on, but he was fobbed off with the usual bullshit and daybook record entries.

'Paul Connolly? Oh, dear. Violent little boy, with a terrible temper. I see he's been throwing himself at the wall again. A bit of a problem, really. We do the best we can, but…'

Again, the power of the written word. You know the phrase 'written in stone'? That's how it works, if you're illiterate and up against others who are out to do you down.

As soon as the carers' version was put in writing, it was halfway to being fact. We could protest and whine and show our bruises – real physical evidence – but there'd always be something written down in the daybook to explain it all away. It was their word against ours, and the result was always going to be the same: Literate Child Abusers 2, Illiterate Kids 0.

It was only years later, when the accident happened and put an end to my dreams of a boxing career, that I discovered that learning to read and write was something I really needed to tackle.

As I worked my way back to health, over nearly two years, I gradually realised that I was learning a lot about myself and even more about how bodies worked. I'd already gathered a fair bit of practical knowledge about fitness and exercise from the hard training I'd done at the boxing club over the years. Nobody gets to be a successful amateur without putting in hundreds of hours a year, in the ring and out of it, and I'd been skipping and running, pumping iron and punching bags for at least thirteen years. The trainers knew their business and I'd learned a lot from them.

Now I was learning new stuff from my conversations with the doctors. The long exercise sessions gave me lots of time to think and I was talking to the physios at every opportunity. *Why are you doing this? What does that do? How can we strengthen other parts of my shoulder to compensate for the deltoid muscle that was destroyed in the accident?*

I was full of questions, and fascinated by the answers. But I always came back to the same old problem. There is only so much you or I, or anybody, can hold on to.

Memory has its limits. That's why we need writing, so that we can put things out there to refer back to, and not have to carry all our knowledge around in our heads.

I needed that. I needed to be able to read and write. I was motivated, determined, dead set on doing it. Yet, when it came to it, it was the hardest thing I had ever done.

I know it's not easy to teach adults things like reading and writing and languages. And I know it's never going to be possible for grown-ups to learn in the simple, free and easy way that young kids do. Tackling adult literacy is a huge challenge. But God, having seen it for myself, I'm sure there must be better ways of going about it.

Dealing with people who are illiterate costs the country a lot of money. Supporting them, scraping them up when something's gone wrong, arresting and jailing them when their frustrations boil over and they do something antisocial – it all costs. So society has a really solid economic interest in helping every single person it can to get those basic tools of reading and writing sorted out. It's actually good business to invest in saving people from illiteracy, as people like Sue Porto at Beanstalk keep on trying to tell governments and anyone else who will listen. I was more than willing to invest in myself, but that didn't make it any easier.

When I had my Ali Moment and decided reading was going to be a must, I signed up as soon as possible for adult literacy classes at night school. It took a lot of effort just to go in and book my place on a class. But that was nothing compared with the mixture of terror and embarrassment that came with me as I headed for the first lesson. And even that was not as bad as the feeling of wanting to run away when the time for the second class came round.

Now I knew what it was going to be like – how hard it would be for me, how out of place I felt, how humiliating the whole process was – I was very close to not going back at all. The building was tatty and smelt of paint, the teachers seemed bored or resigned, rather than inspiring, and my fellow students all seemed to be one sandwich short of a picnic. Perhaps they were all just overwhelmed, like I was, but they struck me as sullen, dull and painfully slow. Looking around, I felt like Einstein, by comparison. And it certainly wasn't because I was making any great progress.

As always, of course, when you make a snap judgement about a group of strangers, I got it wrong – at least in part. Most of the class did seem as if they were there because someone had nudged them inside with a cattle prod, but there were a couple of quite bright sparks. We tended to clump together, and as I got to know them, I found out their stories and how they had slipped through the net and arrived in adulthood without basic literacy skills.

Some, like me, had lived in failing institutions, where learning took second place to survival. Some were from immigrant families and had arrived in this country halfway through their schooling with little or no English. Some had missed many months or years of school through illness, or been dragged from school to school by parents who moved around a lot. Some were bright but dyslexic. Some had obvious learning difficulties or mental health problems.

Most of the teachers were clearly depressed by the task

in front of them, and I felt some were just plain patronising, which I didn't like at all. If you can't stand the heat, I thought, don't take the salary. And don't take it out on the people in front of you. There was one star, though, Grace, who was quick to realise how much it meant to me to get out of the illiteracy trap.

'You're more than ready for it, Paul, and it's really not as difficult as it seems,' she said, after two or three lessons. 'If you do your best and apply yourself, I can help you and you'll be able to learn quite quickly.'

That was a vital factor – that support through the first stages. Grace knew I could do it, and she made me feel she must be right. She avoided showing any favouritism in the lessons, but she'd meet me for coffee between classes and set me little exercises. It took me nearly two years to get my reading and writing up to a reasonable basic standard, but I still remember the quick wins Grace made sure I enjoyed in the early stages – just spelling out the headline on the front of *The Sun* or reading a sale sign in a shop window. I gave her a namecheck in *Against All Odds* and I hope that made her proud. I owe her a lot. Her optimism kept me going when I could easily have given up.

As I started to get over the first hurdles and felt I was making progress, I decided I'd take on another course, in basic computing. Computers made sense to me almost immediately. I liked the logic and there was useful training for me in arithmetic and numeracy skills, which came as part of the course. And I soon found another reason to feel better about going to the classes. There was a good-looking woman in her mid–thirties who'd caught my eye and we drifted into an energetic, undemanding relationship. She was married and seemingly settled and happy at home. All she wanted from me was a good-humoured shag, with no strings attached, and the arrangement brightened up both the classes themselves and our twice-weekly revision meetings in between. I'm not sure how much my computing skills developed after the first few weeks, but I began to feel that adult education wasn't all hard graft.

The very first door that being able to read and write opened for me was being able to study for something more relevant than my computing commitments. You can't study if you can't read. I'd always been fit, and worked at it, because of the boxing. I'd taken in as much as I could from my hundreds of hours of conversation with the doctors and the physios who'd worked so hard to put me back together and help me get in shape again. Now I wanted to put all those elements together and make a career for myself as a professional fitness instructor.

There was a recognised qualification, Fitness for Industry's FFI certificate, and I wanted to get that under my belt. If I could get certified, that would open up the chance of working in the many health and fitness clubs that were starting to open up, first in the trendy parts of the big cities and later right across the country.

For the first time since my dreams of a career in boxing were dashed, opportunity knocked. After a shattering near-death experience and two years building my body back to fitness and getting the monkey of illiteracy off my shoulder, I was ready to grab whatever was coming my way.

CHAPTER 14

ON THE DOORS

As I got back to full fitness, I combined studying and developing my career as a trainer with working on door security for pubs and clubs. I was good at it. It didn't scare me and it brought in a bit of dosh.

A mate told me recently that Pope Francis used to work as a bouncer at nightclubs in Buenos Aires in the 1950s. I checked it, and it's true, apparently. But I have to say there were a lot of things going on in the nightspots of London and Essex in the eighties and nineties that wouldn't have got his blessing. It was the Wild West, and it sometimes got way out of control.

Usually governments don't want to know about what happens on a Friday night, when the people come out to play. But the mayhem was so bad that eventually the politicians stepped in and regulated the door security industry. From 2003 on, 'door supervisors' had to be licensed, with criminal record checks and a minimum of thirty hours' training covering the law, first aid, fire safety and non-violent conflict resolution techniques.

In my day, though, it wasn't quite like that. When I was on the doors, for seventeen years, on and off, it was much more of a free-for-all. Powerful people ran the doors then and you had to know who was who. Your apprenticeship wasn't so much about learning health and safety procedures, it was more about learning the trade – learning who the important faces were, who not to upset and who was allowed to get away with what. There was a lot of politics involved and it could be dangerous to get it wrong.

As a result, the first few months on the door were usually the most difficult. You learned by your early mistakes, and if you survived you got a reputation for being good at the job. Once I'd been in the business for a while, I became pretty well known.

I stood out because I was smaller than most of the other doormen, because I was fit and more or less fearless (which may have been because I carried some sort of death wish) and because of the missing finger on my right hand, the legacy of my fall from the roof in Upminster. All doormen around the world operate under nicknames – that's how the young Mark Vincent turned into Vin Diesel, while he was working at nightclubs in New York, before fame struck – and inevitably, I suppose, they called me Fingers. I didn't like the name, because it made me sound like a pickpocket. But the more I didn't like it, the harder it stuck, first among my friends and then among my enemies, too.

Door staff used working names because you never knew when you might need to disappear. A nickname made you harder to trace. And while many of them might be unflattering, cartoon-like labels, they were often accurate descriptions. Billy Big Arms was so pumped up from all the weights he did that he had to have his jackets made specially, with extra-wide sleeves. Nicky No-Neck really looked the part. I never met Vin Diesel, but the 'diesel' bit was apparently a reference to his relentless, non-stop energy, though he was also built like a truck.

One of the biggest problems for us was weapons. You had to pat people down and take their weapons away from them – and sometimes they might resent that. One place I worked at, a club in Forest Gate, was really rough. I was there for a couple of years in my late twenties and that place was a baptism of fire for me.

You'd go to work each evening just knowing there'd be trouble. It wasn't if, but when. Working on the door there, you were taking knives off people every night and every now and again there'd be guns as well. People would get very touchy about the guns. We'd risk life and limb taking them off them, and then the police would come swinging by at about one o'clock in the morning and pick up all the weapons we'd collected for them.

There were a lot of guns around, especially in the early nineties, when Yugoslavia had fallen apart. With the war going on over there, there were all kinds of Serbs and Albanians and Bosnians in London, with a hell of a lot of guns. And there were drug wars here and gang wars, so a lot of people were carrying firearms.

You'd see people queuing up to come in and you'd pat them down. They all knew we'd be under orders not to let them in carrying a gun, but some of them might think the doorman would be too scared to take it away. That sometimes happened, especially with the less experienced youngsters. Or someone would bring a little gun, a Saturday night special, and try to smuggle it in, hidden under his crotch. Pat too near there and they'd get very arsy.

For the guy on the door, guns were always a problem. When you were patting some bloke down and there was a gun there, you had a choice. And you had no more than two or three seconds to make it, knowing the wrong decision could end up in a very nasty situation. There was no rule book about what to do next, except that if you'd taken a gun, you never returned it.

If you found one and took it off someone, the conversation would almost always be the same.

'All right, mate. No trouble. Give me my gun back and I'll go.'

'Sorry, can't do that. We can't give it back to you now, now we've got it.'

At that point, anything could happen.

People would often give up a knife without making too much fuss. A gun was different. Sometimes they'd slink away and you wouldn't see them again. Sometimes things would kick off and you'd have a real fight on your hands in a matter of seconds. Sometimes they'd go and then come back again to take revenge. My friend Chrissie was shot dead on the door at a club in Ilford. Some little Jamaican from South London came back and just stuck an automatic pistol in the door, pulled the trigger and sprayed the foyer with bullets. Chrissie was unlucky that night and he got one in the head.

Altogether, four of the guys I worked with were killed

working on the door. We wore bulletproof jackets, of course, but that didn't always protect you. I worked for a while for my mate, Kimber, at a big jungle club in Stratford. That was a huge place, an old movie theatre, and there were fifty doormen employed to keep the peace – or at least move the fighting outside. One of my colleagues there was shot dead on the front door because he wouldn't let a drug dealer in. The guy was trying to get money off a promoter who owed him for a deal that had gone wrong. But that doorman was really out of luck. The bullet that killed him hit his elbow, ricocheted off and went in through the side of his bulletproof vest, under the armpit, and straight into his heart. If the killer hadn't been such a lousy shot, the jacket would have saved him.

I remember one huge black guy who really wanted his gun back. He forced his way past all of us and raced up three flights of stairs after the head doorman, who was taking the pistol to put it in the safe. The head doorman, an older man, knew he was coming all right, but he just went on up the stairs, with the big lump gaining on him all the time. Right at the top, just as the other guy was catching up with him, he turned and hit him with a single punch, right on the button. It knocked him out cold, and we watched this big fucker fall, bumping all the way down the stairs again.

Guns were just not that rare then. Wherever you went, there was the potential for trouble, and I accidentally provoked plenty one night down at a club in Vauxhall. I was doing my job conscientiously and I'd taken a load of drugs off a dealer. But I didn't realise who he was working for and he came back with his mates for a drive-by shooting, with several of them blazing away at all of us in the doorway. There six of us, all the rest of them much bigger than me, and we were all scrambling over each other to get through that door at the same time, like something out of the Keystone Cops. The dealer and his mates were using sawn-off shotguns and we were wearing bulletproof jackets, so we were hurt, rather than seriously injured. But when people are firing and it's coming in your direction, you don't want to hang around to see if it's shot or bullets.

The next time I was face-to-face with a shotgun, it was at much closer range. One night I was working at an East End club when two serious people turned up. I knew who they were, but it was two in the morning and my head doorman had told me very firmly not to let anyone else in. So I said no, and they took it badly. One of them was wearing a long coat and he opened it discreetly, a few inches, so I could see the shotgun nestled inside. Nothing that would show on the CCTV pictures, mind, but quite enough to get the message across.

He wasn't pleased that I'd stopped him and he said so, in no uncertain terms.

'See you, you little cunt. I'll blow your fucking head right off. Don't you know who I am?'

I did, and that was the trouble. Non-violent conflict resolution seemed like the best approach.

'Course I know who you are. And I'm not disrespecting you, but you know who I work for – and he's told me I can't let you in.'

The hard man twitched the coat open again and I heard a gasp from my buddy on the door – a proper martial arts expert, but a new and inexperienced doorman. He'd just seen the gun and clocked this guy's manner and he was rigid with fear. As we stood there for the next few seconds, he just lost it and wet himself. He was literally standing there in a puddle of piss. Then, with surprising speed for a man with wet trousers, he bolted into the darkness and never came back. We never saw him again. I guess £50 a night was not enough to tempt him after seeing that gun.

So I was left, on my own, walking a very fine line. I nudged the red panic alarm on the right of the doorframe and hoped the right person would see the flashing light inside and come out.

The next minute seemed like an hour. I was playing for time and hoping for reinforcements. The hard man was getting more annoyed, and I had no doubt he'd carry out his threat if he felt pissed off enough. He'd probably enjoy it, too.

'Well?' he growled.

'You know it's not me,' I said. 'You know who's in charge here. It's more than my life's worth…'

'No. You don't understand. Getting in my way is what's more than your fucking life's worth, you little prick. You get me?'

This guy was angry, and it was starting to get personal.

'You're not going to look so pretty once I blow your fucking face off, you little cunt.'

That was it, I reckoned. Enough of the formalities. Next up, he'd do something.

You could have heard a pin drop. Instead, I heard a step behind me and felt a chest against my back.

Hallelujah! Desmond.

'Is there a problem here? Can I help?' asked Desmond.

Straight away, you could see the shotgun was suddenly irrelevant.

It was instant and miraculous. Peace broke out. Tension gone, the four of us chatted in the foyer and the two unwelcome guests said goodbye and went off into the night. It was the Law of the Jungle in its purest form. He was a serious face in his own right, Desmond, and the big guy just had to pull his neck in. Desmond was definitely in his league and maybe a bit higher.

That night was a good example of the subtle hierarchy that ruled that world. Desmond was a proper face, but a lot of head doormen were just the people put up to front a place. Often you would find that the people who really ran things were one or two of the other doormen inside, and you had to be in the know to have any idea where the real power was.

Even in those days, doormen never carried guns. It just wouldn't work. If something does go badly wrong, it's hard to stand up in court and claim that the gun you suddenly happened to find in your hand is a defensive weapon. There was obviously a violent side to what we had to do, but, believe it or not, less trouble was always preferable to more.

Still, it was a dangerous way to earn a living. You needed something to fall back on if a fight got out of hand. Sometimes we'd have a cosh, in case things got really ugly, or the doorman would carry a CS spray, which are good for sorting out situations without raising the stakes too high. London's bouncers were pioneers in the use of these little CS spray cans. They were highly illegal, of course, but useful because they could stop a bull in its tracks without causing any lasting damage. Many doormen had been equipped with them, very discreetly, for years before the police came round to the same way of thinking and adopted CS sprays, for exactly the same reasons, in 1996.

But the weapon of last resort, the one nobody talks about, was the old-fashioned knuckleduster. When a doorman was isolated, on his own and surrounded by guys who wanted to do him some serious damage, all he had left in his pocket was his knuckleduster.

Dusters are fucking lethal. They turn a punch into something far more serious. You can break ribs with a single blow to the body. If you hit someone hard to the head, you'd probably kill them. Getting your duster out is like pressing the red button and going nuclear. But if you're literally fighting for your life and it's really you or them, you do what you have to do. 'Better to be tried by twelve than carried by six,' my old friend Ronnie Redruff used to say. Dead is never the best option. In practical terms, dusters had other advantages, too. CCTV cameras don't pick up that kind of detail and you could unload them off on a friend or get rid of them unobtrusively before the cops turned up.

I carried a duster for seventeen years, and I used it just once in all that time. I'm not going to go into details, but I can't bring myself to regret that, because I have no doubt it saved my life.

CHAPTER 15

SEX AND FAMILIES

Life was getting complicated and my hands were more than full. I was pretty hard and handsome, well-toned and fit, and I always felt I was in with a chance if a good-looking girl caught my eye. My personal training career was going along nicely, so there was a bit of money around and I was feeling cocky enough to go for it.

As a result, I was in danger of wearing myself out. I was juggling two women, both pretty gorgeous, both pretty demanding and both – to be fair – fully aware that they were not the only one. In fact, despite what people think, I've generally found that lots of women are just as ready as men to enjoy a full-on fuck, without worrying too much about what's going to happen the next day. And if they were up for it, so was I. I didn't keep a diary, but I sometimes needed a pretty good memory to remember where I was supposed to be and who I was supposed to be with on any particular night.

I've come across people in the past who've been unsympathetic to the various troubles that twisted the early part of my life.

'The world doesn't owe you a living,' they say.

Well, no. They're right. It doesn't owe me a living, and I've always been willing to work hard to earn the dosh I need. But I did always have a sneaking feeling that the world did owe me a shagging.

Despite growing up in the warped sexual hothouse of St Leonard's, where every kind of sexual encounter – fumbling, loving, straight or gay, casual, multiple, brutal, abusive, forced and paedophilic – seemed to be going on all the time, I had not had my first fuck until I was almost seventeen. It wasn't that I was shy or prudish. I was certainly looking forward to 'having it off', as we so delicately put it, at the earliest opportunity. I suppose it was usually just a case of not being in the right place at the right time.

The first time I ever came close, that's all that happened. A false start, to put it politely. I was thirteen and I managed to convince myself I was in love with a bright, lively girl in our cottage called Maria. She had long, loose Mediterranean curls and a slim, taut little body, with deep, dark eyes and smooth olive-brown skin. We got on well, and it gradually seemed to be going further than that. She seemed to like me, too, and I wanted more.

Like all the boys, I'd had a couple of educational encounters with the girls – just touching and feeling and envying the others who boasted about having 'gone all the way'. There were a couple of girls who would go over the park with a whole gang of boys and egg us all on to do our worst. At the time, it didn't occur to me that there was anything sad about wanting warmth and approval that much. I'd wait my turn in the queue and copy what the others seemed to be doing, but I'd never done it, as such.

With Maria, I was feeling a very special attraction. There was some danger involved in sneaking along the landing, past the carers' bedrooms, to the girls' dormitory at the other end. If Uncle Bill happened to get up for a pee and catch me creeping past, he'd beat the shit out of me. But I was used to that. It was almost part of my routine. And I wanted to see Maria.

I slipped along the creaking landing and tiptoed in, hoping I hadn't misread Maria's signals. I hadn't, and she pulled me to her, warm and smooth in her little nightie, with those long bare legs against mine.

'Come on,' she whispered. 'Come here.'

She kissed me and I realised I'd never been kissed properly before. She held me against her and ran her hands down my sides. I thought I would burst with joy.

'Come on, Paul,' she said. 'Do it.'

It wasn't that I didn't want to. And I had a pretty good idea what it involved. It was just that everything seemed to be happening very fast. Too fast. I was holding her against me and fumbling with my pyjamas when suddenly it all got out of hand. Badly.

'Oh, no!'

'What's the matter?'

'Maria. I've got to go. I'm sorry. I've just… I've just… Er, I've just got to go.'

I fled back, past the carers' doors, into the safety of the boys' room.

'That didn't take long, you dirty cunt,' a voice said from the darkness.

'Get fucked,' I muttered, and buried my head under the pillow.

For the next few days, I kept out of the way of Maria and all the rest of the girls, as much as I could. They'd have kept on at her till she told them what had happened. My name would be mud, or something worse. And the spell had been broken. She was actually all right about it, eventually, but it kind of put me off.

Partly because of that, I suppose, I was the last person I knew to lose my virginity. Once I had found out which way was up, at the hands of a highly experienced girl who wasn't going to take no for answer, I set about making up for lost time. They say the best things in life are free and I quickly discovered that there was nothing quite as enjoyable as that amazing feeling of being caught up in the moment. For the next twenty years or so, I shagged every good-looking girl who came my way – and a lot of others I'd rather not think about now.

I had a couple of fairly serious girlfriends at various times, including my first true head-over-heels romance, with the lovely Lindsey, daughter of a local police sergeant.

In fact, as it turned out, I had a whole series of relationships that brought me into close contact with the law, in the nicest possible way. At least three of my girlfriends, over the years, were serving police officers. One of the best, Anthea, really did me a favour by turning up and supporting me, day after day, when I was up in court facing my serious GBH charges, despite the fact that we'd split up long before then. It wasn't necessarily that I liked women in uniform. To be honest, I liked them more out of uniform. But I think there was something about the strength and self-confidence of some of these women that appealed to me – and they were undeniably fit.

I was learning about life, and people, and catching up after my slow start.

Eventually, years later, I even got married. Kim and I had one of those relationships that starts off like a blazing comet, but leaves you both wondering, after the fires have burned down, what on earth you ever had in common. Before, after, and sometimes during, those relationships I would chase, and usually catch, all kinds of women. To be fair, it wasn't always my fault. A lot of the women didn't run very fast when they saw I was after them.

But by the time I met Jo, I had completely given up on any romantic notion of finding true love forever and a partner for life. Even when I finally bumped into her, at the club where I was working as a personal trainer, I thought she was just a hot, fit twenty-five-year-old bird who might be persuaded to spend some time having a bit of fun. She was fourteen years younger than me, but I offered her a free training session, followed by an invitation to join me at a Valentine's Day party given by some very good friends of mine, Susan and Kevin McCabe. The McCabes were Americans. They were millionaire bankers and they lived in a luxurious modern flat right by the Thames at Butler's Wharf, so I guessed Jo might be rather impressed by the people I rubbed shoulders with. To be fair, if she'd met some of my other mates that night, she'd probably have run a mile.

The party went well, though, and by the time we had followed up with a more down-to-earth date or two, we were getting in deep.

There was still the little matter of the other girls I mentioned at the beginning of this chapter. They both had their particular attractions and I was loath to disappoint them.

One was a lovely bird, a swimming coach and extremely athletic. The other was something of an exhibitionist and particularly dedicated to making phone calls interesting. But I didn't find phone sex a particular turn-on, especially when I was driving in heavy traffic. I'd warn her that I had a car full of mates and that I was going to put the call on loudspeaker, but that wouldn't make her ring off. I don't know if she ever believed me that there were four of us in the car, but I don't think she cared anyway, and my mates were grateful for the entertainment.

Jo seemed like something very important, right from the off, and it quickly became clear to me that Jo-plus-2 was not a workable situation. I guess the other two girls might have put up with that – they'd both got used to the idea that they were not my one-and-only. But as soon as things got serious with Jo, I realised I had to stop seeing the others.

I'd had a lot of practice, over the years, at being the lad about town, the hard nut with a soft touch for the ladies. Now I was going to have to give up what had really been my hobby. Drink and drugs had never really appealed to me, and since I'd stopped throwing my weight around and getting into fights, I had pretty well dedicated my time to working, training and sex.

But when Jo came into my life, there was a whole lot more to think about. Once I'd found her and begun to realise how lucky I'd got, I wasn't going to let this amazing person get away from me. She was young, pretty, tough and extremely moral, with a very strong sense of right and wrong. She was also incredibly loyal. In public, she was great. She'd stand up for me, whatever the circumstances. But when we were alone together, she'd stand toe-to-toe with me and make me back down whenever I wanted to do stupid things.

Being with Jo made me want to be a better person. I could feel myself becoming more thoughtful, less tense, happier. I felt great about my life and our relationship, but then, of course, I began to worry whether that was just me going soft. It wasn't. I worked as hard as ever, did as much, stayed as fit. It was just that I no longer had this rather desperate energy driving me on all the time, as if the world would come to an end if I took my eye off the ball.

I think I can safely say that the idea of becoming a father, of starting a family, had never occurred to me as a serious possibility. I wasn't the type. Besides I didn't know what fathers did, as I hadn't had one of my own to study or been able to borrow and watch anyone else's. When my friend Mary Littler got married and she and Adrian had a son, I was able to see some glimpses of what a good father might be like. But then, in my years of self-disgust, I had broken off contact with Mary and her family. I hadn't seen them for two decades, from my teens to mid-thirties. For a very long time, there was not a single family I could focus on as a good example of what family life might be like.

Now I was with Jo and we were going to make one. It

was, in many ways, the most terrifying adventure of my life. In terms of how vulnerable it makes you, having children and feeling so responsible for their health, happiness and wellbeing, it still is.

CHAPTER 16

WRITING THE BOOK

As I started to realise that I had a new life, with a new me, as a secure, happy family man with a loving wife and two growing boys, a proper home and a successful business of my own, I began to look at my past differently. Instead of seeing my childhood just as a nightmare I must struggle to leave behind, I began to feel that I could look it squarely in the eye.

My suffering at the hands of the abusers at St Leonard's was not unique, after all. There had been 300 children at the home at any one time, so that meant my experience must have been shared with who knows how many other kids. I was there throughout the 1970s, but Uncle Bill Starling and Alan Prescott had been there before I arrived, and it wasn't till 1984 that Tower Hamlets council closed down the home and sold the site for redevelopment.

Suddenly, it hit me. The story had not been told.

There had been a brief flurry of newspaper coverage at

the time of the trial, in 2001, though only the *Guardian* and a few local papers had given it any space. But there were no books about it. Nobody knew what had been going on. No one had told the world about the constant physical and mental bullying and brutality. Even the details of the sexual abuse at The Drive had been limited to what could be proved in court, and that was only the tip of a very big iceberg. There was no record at all, from the child's point of view, of what our awful lives had been like.

Apart from Bill Starling's fourteen-year prison sentence and the few months Prescott had spent on remand before his conviction – and the isolated conviction of Haydn Davies for buggery, way back in the early 1980s, when he'd obviously been seen as just one bad apple – no one had been put behind bars. The long and expensive police investigation, known as Operation Mapperton, had clearly established that rampant abuse had taken place over many years. After all, in his public statement after the court case, Detective Inspector Daniel O'Malley had confirmed that there had been 'systematic child abuse' at St Leonard's. The police investigation had also revealed the shocking truth that only two boys from our dorm at Wallis Cottage, Maxwell and myself, had survived to reach the age of thirty-five.

But the fact that so many witnesses were dead had made prosecution difficult, and the police admitted that videos of several key witness statements had gone missing, whatever that meant. So that, as far as the criminal justice system was concerned, was the end of the line. No one, it seemed, was interested enough to push it further.

The more I thought about this, the angrier I got. Was

the public really not interested in knowing what the children had to say? If people didn't know or care about the abuse of my generation of kids in a council-run home, how alert would they be to things that might be going on right now? Somebody ought to tell our story. And I suddenly realised that somebody was going to have to be me.

Once the penny dropped, I decided that I must do my absolute best to tell the world the truth about what it had been like, growing up in St Leonard's. I had no idea how to do it, but I knew I'd need some help.

Putting myself in the role of the author seemed like a bad bit of miscasting, but maybe I could find someone – a collaborator or co-author, or a ghostwriter – who could help me capture all the things I needed to say and shape it all into a book. I wasn't illiterate any more, but writing anything lengthy was like pulling teeth for me. And I certainly didn't have the skills to structure the material and make it work.

I was working sixty hours a week as a personal trainer, so using a ghostwriter was probably the only way to get the book done before I was old and grey – and before it was too late to re-open the investigation into the goings-on at St Leonard's.

The other advantage was that it can be easier to tell a story like this to and through someone you don't really know. It was always going to be difficult for me to be objective about my own life and at this stage I couldn't bear the thought of going through the story of my harrowing childhood with my wife or a close friend.

I didn't want to offload all that shit onto Jo, especially as we have always avoided talking about the ugly details. It would be a burden for her, I know, and I have enough trouble carrying it myself sometimes. There have been whole periods of my life when it's been like a hunched devil on my back, pressing me down and whispering evil things in my ear. But it's my load to carry, and nobody else's.

As the interviews with the ghostwriter went on and the questions became more probing and personal, I was shocked at my reaction to the opening up of these old wounds. As the memories were dredged to the surface, the nightmares began. I would get through the interview sessions all right, but in the early hours – at two or maybe three o'clock in the morning – the trouble would start.

I began waking up abruptly, streaming with sweat and screaming so loud that I woke up Jo and Harley, who was just five and probably thought the world was coming to an end. Jo was pregnant with Archie, our second son, at the time and my nightly turmoil was the last thing she needed. Knowing I was ruining her sleep made me feel even worse and I hated myself for reacting like this, when my greatest wish was to be strong and protective of my family.

I moved downstairs to sleep on the sofa until it all blew over, trying all the time to push the violent emotions back down, deep into my subconscious. I was used to living with my own personal demon on my back and I'd got so comfortable with him being there that I'd given up trying to shake him off. For years, I would just rearrange things until the burden felt a bit lighter and get on with life as usual. Now that this wouldn't work, I felt as if I was going mad.

I've done enough therapy sessions over the years to

know full well that I was going through a natural process and that I shouldn't have been embarrassed about my reactions to raking up old agonies. In my head, I knew it was a normal response. The feelings I'd had as a child and a young man hadn't gone away. Now these zombie emotions were rising up from where they had been buried and coming out to haunt me. I didn't have a way to get rid of them, so I'd just have to tough it out. I kept busy, busy, busy during the day, in the hope that I'd be out for the count by the time I laid my head down. And, of course, it didn't really work like that. I was becoming a pale, hollow-eyed, dog-tired zombie myself. For a few weeks, I must have been pretty close to the edge.

The change I'd been praying for came as the first chapters of the book began to take shape. I started to be able to read my own life story as a narrative, almost as if it was about someone else. I concentrated on making sure the details were accurate and nothing important was missing, and gradually it became easier to focus on painful episodes and put them into context. I'd go through the draft chapters, sometimes with Jo, always with my best mate Ian, and OK them or amend them until they told it like it was. It took five months' work to get a manuscript we felt we could send out to publishers, and it wasn't over a moment too soon.

What happened next was surprising and exciting. For one thing, the last of the nightmares decided to call it a day. That was a big improvement. I was fed up with the sofa. Now I didn't have to keep thinking about my shitty childhood, the pressure seemed to ease a little, leaving me more like my usual self.

But the other development came as a real surprise. We'd worked out a list of publishers to send details of the book to, in the hope of getting a deal, and I'd been warned by people who know that there were likely to be a lot of disappointments before we found someone to take it on. So I wasn't expecting to hit the jackpot first time. That's not a financial term here – no one makes money out of writing books these days, except J.K. Rowling and that *50 Shades of Grey* woman. But the very first people we approached about my book, John Blake Publishing, came back with the offer I was hoping for. That doesn't happen, but it just did.

Suddenly, destiny was smiling on me. Now I knew I would get a chance to tell the world what had happened to the children at St Leonard's while the authorities weren't looking. I'd be able to make up for not having killed the paedophiles when they were in my sights and to pay my own tribute to the kids who didn't survive to make new lives for themselves.

I had no idea if people would notice my little paperback, or if it would sink without trace in a market that sees 150,000 new books each year. And at that stage, in mid-2009, I'd never even seen an ebook. But I was excited to think that my story of growing up in St Leonard's would be published and put out there for anyone who happened to take an interest.

It was a turning point, obviously. I could see that. But there was no way I could ever have imagined all the things, good and bad, that would happen to me in the next year or two.

CHAPTER 17

RAMSDEN HALL

When the paperback edition of *Against All Odds* came out, it didn't immediately set the Thames on fire. It sold pretty well, though, and I was very proud that I actually had a book out, when I'd only ever read one in my life – from cover to cover, anyway. That was Muhammad Ali's autobiography, *The Greatest*, the amazing story of his rise from a semi-illiterate dunce to the top of the world. I found that inspiring. He was – and always will be – my Number One hero. You only have to walk into my house to be confronted straight away by my precious black-and-white Ali photo, signed by him back in the early days when he was still Cassius Clay.

So I was more surprised than anyone when the Kindle ebook edition of *Against All Odds*, which came out more than a year later, took off like a rocket. The media homed in on the new revelations about the mental, physical and sexual abuse that went unchecked at the St Leonard's children's home and I was soon doing lots of radio and press interviews.

As word of mouth about the book spread, it climbed to the top of Amazon's Kindle charts, even outselling books like *The Girl With the Dragon Tattoo*. When it hit Number One, it was Christmas. I had no idea anything was going on till the phone rang in my kitchen.

'This is John Blake,' a voice said. 'The office is closed for the holidays, so I thought I'd ring you myself to let you know your book is right at the top of the bestseller charts.'

'Yeah, right. Happy Christmas. Fuck off!' I said, and put the phone down.

I've got a handful of mates who like to wind people up with prank phone calls every now and again. I don't mind a laugh, but Christmas is always busy for me, what with all the women trying to get into shape at the last minute to fit into their little black party dresses. I didn't have time for that sort of shit.

'Bloody hell,' I said to Jo, 'Some people don't know when to give it a rest.'

'Who was it?' she asked.

'Dunno. Someone taking the piss out of me about the book. Fuck them.'

The phone rang again and I picked it up, expecting it to be my mate calling back. I got ready to read the riot act.

'Excuse me, old boy,' said the voice. 'I *am* John Blake, of John Blake Publishing, and your book *is* a bestseller. And I really don't think you should swear at me, especially when I'm bringing good news.'

When I came off the phone, Jo and I went online to see

if it was true. I still wasn't convinced the plummy voice on the line really was my publishing company's MD.

There was the Amazon Kindle chart. And there was *Against All Odds*, right at the top.

'My God,' said Jo. 'It's true!'

I just stared at the screen.

'I don't fucking believe it.' I said.

'So what happens now?' Jo asked.

'Fuck knows. We'll just have to wait and see.'

What happened next, of course, was that the journos all went mad for it again. Now they all wanted to do the same story – about how this kid who'd managed to grow up unable to read and write had suddenly become a bestselling author. Because I'd had to go through the struggle and embarrassment of taking adult reading classes in my late twenties, I became a sort of champion for the charities and other bodies who try to help with adult literacy and the care of underprivileged children.

At first, it was more or less accidental. People who worked with literacy problems or cared for vulnerable kids started to refer to my book or me and quote my story to prove all sorts of different points. I was happy with that, but I didn't really do anything about it for a while. But then some of these people started to get in touch with me to ask if I could help more actively. One of them was the head of a local school, Ramsden Hall, just a few minutes up the road from my home in Essex. When she picked up the phone, she really started something.

Ramsden Hall looks after boys with special behavioural, emotional and educational needs – tough, disturbed kids with a lot of different problems. The woman who made the call to me introduced herself as Yvonne Goouge. She told me that a couple of her teachers had read *Against All Odds* and decided it should have a place on the curriculum. They had started using my book in lessons to show the students that, even if you come from a tough background, there are things you can do to make sure your life works out OK. It may seem like you've been dealt a bad hand – and maybe you have – but that doesn't mean you've got to sit there and just suck it up.

Yvonne asked me if I would go there and address the school assembly.

'Your book's been a huge hit round here,' she explained, 'We've seen some kids' behaviour really change after they've read it. It'd be fantastic if you could come and talk to them in person.'

I said I'd go along and see what I could do, but I didn't have much idea what that might be.

The boys who end up at Ramsden Hall have usually been kicked out of every other school. But they're difficult for a reason. Many of them are from very deprived backgrounds and have already been through the wars in a big way. They can be rude and violent, troubled and unpleasant. A lot have been diagnosed as having this or that kind of attention deficit disorder, while some are on heavy medication all the time. Some already have criminal convictions.

These boys have very low self-esteem and tend to lash out with frustration. They haven't learned to control their tempers or even delay their reactions long enough to respond in any other way. Half the time you want to give them a hug; the other half you want to pick up one in each hand and bang their fucking heads together.

I liked Yvonne's approach. She said my book would stay on the curriculum – despite all the swearwords, descriptions of violence and stories of baddies and brothels – because it's something these boys can relate to and it's written the way they talk. They're not going to be shocked by a bit of cursing and swearing or by accounts of prostitution and criminality. In some cases, they might well be reading about people from their own backgrounds.

When the day came for me to give my talk, I realised I was actually feeling more nervous at Ramsden Hall than when I was giving my big speech to the movers and shakers at the House of Lords. Facing me was a mass of studiously bored teenage faces. These boys were not going to be easy to impress. A few days before, a bunch of the little Herberts had let off steam by burning down a neighbouring farmer's barn, so I was playing to a tough audience that was tuned in to action, rather than words.

But the kids were obviously surprised by what I'd got to say and they had plenty of questions they wanted to ask. When I looked at those boys, I could see myself at their age, forty years ago. I was just the same. Hurt, angry and aggressive, I'd push people away. I'd never learned to put my negative feelings into words – and I'd had no one to talk to anyway.

'Mister,' one of the boys asked at the end, 'How do you manage to just leave when someone's trying to beat you up?'

Good question. I explained that it wasn't always easy, but with a lot of deep breaths and focus I can now walk away, even when someone's really asking for it.

'Mister,' asked another, 'When you were working at the

brothels, did you ever want to get your leg over with one of the prossies?'

I moved swiftly on.

Of course I did, but I hadn't taken some vow to tell these boys everything.

Boxing was a favourite topic, and they asked me all about it. Then they wanted to know how I'd become a trainer, what it was like meeting celebrities and Hollywood stars and how I'd got round to writing a book. You could see they found it hard to imagine ending up like me – gainfully employed, not in trouble with the law and leading what the world would think of as a 'normal' life. For them, it was all an endless battle against the system. They couldn't imagine ever paying rent or a mortgage, holding down a job or supporting a family.

Many of the kids asked penetrating questions about the abuse at the children's home and how violent I had really been in the past. They didn't miss much, and I was as honest with them as I could be.

I could see this was all getting them quite involved. I guess they didn't often get to talk to someone like me and I felt I owed them a bit of useful advice.

'You're banging your head against a brick wall if you try to change the system on your own,' I said. 'Bend the rules if you have to, but try and find a place for yourself in society, because that's the only way to get your life sorted out.'

There's no point trying to fight it all alone, I explained, because you'll never win. You can bend some of the rules and you can roll with it, but you won't beat the system. I remembered what I'd been like, so angry with the system that I just wanted to give it the finger and do my own thing. If only there'd been someone to sit me down and explain to me that wouldn't work and I was somehow going to have to find a way to be inside the system myself. If I'd heard that message, it would surely have saved me a lot of heartache.

Not really, of course. Because I'd never have listened.

After that first session with the boys, I couldn't just walk away. Since then I've been doing what I can to generate cash and publicity for Ramsden Hall. I've done things like book signings at local libraries. My posh mate, Ian, won a washing machine at some TV industry gala dinner and donated it to the cause, while my less posh mate, Dave, chipped in with a couple of hundred quid and some boxing equipment to help with a plan I'd come up with.

My idea was to take a few young boxers and trainers in there with me regularly, every month, to give the boys boxing classes but also a little bit of mentoring, just like I'd got from the Dagenham Boxing Club adults when I was a kid. That's what we do now. The boys learn about discipline through the boxing, and they get the chance to see young men, and women, too, who are only a few years older than them and are getting on in the world, running their own training and fitness businesses.

One of their favourites is Sonny. He's a talented boxer and I've had him under my wing for several years now. He's won some pretty important fights and he's had his own training business since he was nineteen. Sonny's in great shape, likeable and easy to talk to, and the kids just idolise him. Never mind all the theory about male role models. They don't just want to be like Sonny. They want to be him.

'Sorry about that,' I tell them. 'The job's taken. But if you make up your mind about what you want and really go for it, you can be you instead and make that work.'

For kids like this, getting across the idea that you can find your own way and your own success is really important. Life doesn't have to be shit.

The key thing is to find out what you're good at or what you love doing and make that your personal goal. Not everyone's going to be able to rise above a bad start and become a brain surgeon or a BA pilot. Not everyone's got the determination to be a sportsman or a fitness trainer, though that can be a way forward for those with a bit of talent. But you don't need to be a big shot to be a success. Just achieving things like a normal job and a happy family is one hell of a success for most of us.

I like the Ramsden Hall kids. I like their spunk and energy and their nose for bullshit. I like their enthusiasm, once you give them something they can relate to. And I think they're pretty lucky to have good people like Yvonne and her staff helping them along, rather than evil bastards like Auntie Coral and Bill Starling grinding them down. Maybe the world has got better over the years.

There are seventy-two boys at that school at any one time. Some may already be damaged beyond repair. But most of those kids can go on to do something, if they're given the chance. Maybe one day I will walk into a local accountancy firm or supermarket or health club and find it being run by some bright young graduate of Ramsden Hall. I'm looking forward to that.

CHAPTER 18

FAMOUS

When *Against All Odds* began to sell thousands of copies and I was on TV and in the papers, people started to recognise me in the street. I was featured in a very popular Channel 4 show called *Who Knows Best?*, in which I did intensive fitness work with a seriously obese woman, competing against an alternative therapist to see who was more effective in helping their client lose weight. It went well and I won, by a mile.

Suddenly, I was 'that bloke off the telly'. I'd be picking the kids up from school or loading up the porridge oats and loo rolls in the supermarket car park and people I'd never seen in my life before would come over and say hello.

Some of them just really liked the idea that an ordinary Essex bloke like me had written a book they could see on the shelves in WH Smith. Some told me how pleased they were that the poor children of St Leonard's had been given a voice at last. Others didn't say much at all but just stood there shaking hands with me, sometimes holding back the tears in a way that made me think they, too, might know a bit about growing up surrounded by pain and violence.

My son, Harley, began to think I was some kind of star and kept telling his friends and schoolmates all about what was going on, which was getting embarrassing.

'I'm not really famous, son,' I tried to tell him. 'Not like Justin Bieber or Miley Cyrus or Boris Johnson. You don't want to get too carried away with what you tell people.'

But Harley wasn't having any of it.

'Yes you are, Dad,' he said. 'People come up to you and want to shake your hand. That means you really are famous.'

We were walking down the High Street one day when a really big, muscle-bound bloke started watching us. I wasn't sure about him. He must have been about six-foot-four, built like a brick shithouse, and there was a time when I'd have confronted him immediately and asked him who he was staring at. But I don't do that now. Over the years I've learned that if someone wants to stare, that's their business. It doesn't do me any harm. So I ignored him as best I could, but my hackles were up and I was definitely on the alert for trouble. After a while, he came up and grabbed my hand.

'Your book,' he said. 'It's… It's amazing! Thanks for writing it.'

I'd have been happy to talk to him, but he turned away almost immediately and I could see he was choking up. My guess is that there was something in his childhood that was a lot like mine and my story had hit him at some very personal level. I muttered a few words but he was away, off, into the crowd. How does someone who's six-foot-four disappear so fast?

'See, Dad,' said Harley. 'Famous. Told you so! I'm really proud of you.'

For me, it was funny to see how strangers behaved differently, just because they'd seen me on television. My fifteen minutes of fame didn't last very long, but for a few weeks the people in the shops were packing all our shopping up for us and generally making a ridiculous fuss of me. To be fair, I wasn't particularly comfortable with all that extra attention, but Harley loved it.

I hardly dared tell him I'd turned down the opportunity to be a lot more famous than that. He's a big fan of *The Only Way Is Essex* and the production company had wanted me to get involved with the show, right back at the time when they were planning the first series. It started with a call from one of the producers.

'We're filming part of our new show about life in Essex up at a local nightclub, and I know you used to be the head doorman there,' the woman said. 'And you've got your fitness training company that's actually called Essex Training. You'd be just right for *TOWIE*.'

'*TOWIE*?' I said. 'What's that?'

'Oh, sorry,' she said. 'It's what we call the show. The full name is *The Only Way Is Essex*.'

I hadn't heard anything about this before, so I asked her to fill me in on what the show would be like.

'Well, it's fun,' she said. 'To be honest, it's mainly about people who've got lots of money and don't know how to spend it. It's kind of reality TV. We'll film them living their lives, in a lot of different situations. We don't really know how it will turn out, but we're hoping for drama, scandal, affairs, all that sort of thing.'

'I can't do that,' I said. 'It's not for me. I'm in my late forties, married with two kids and I've got a respectable business. I wouldn't have a business left if I was in a show like that. Sorry, you've got the wrong guy.'

It's probably the lowest form of celebrity going, that kind of reality TV fame, where you become well-known not for anything you can do but just because the cameras are on you, week after week. I was sure then that if I'd done it, nobody would ever take me seriously again – as a fitness trainer, an author, a public speaker, a campaigner for literacy issues and abused children, or anything else. But I may have been wrong. If you're clever about it, maybe you can make that kind of celebrity work for you and use it as a platform for more important things.

Certainly Harley was appalled when I confessed to him later that I could have been in *TOWIE*.

'You what, Dad?' he said. 'Why didn't you do it? That would have been major! You could have been really famous.'

When I watch my nine-year-old shaping and styling his hair like Joey Essex and putting his calendar up on his bedroom wall, I suppose I wonder if I did the right thing. I even had another chance to ride the bandwagon, when I was asked, a lot later, if I'd do some training for some of the *TOWIE* cast. Again, worries about losing what I'd built up for myself, plus a little bit of snobbery, made me turn it down.

'I've trained two of the biggest female stars in

Hollywood,' I ranted. 'And you want me to train these idiots? Forget it!'

Looking back on it, getting on my high horse like that was almost certainly a mistake. It probably actually hurt me. If the chance came again, I think I'd go for it. I'm more secure now and that was an opportunity missed, but you can't go backwards. And the fact is, I suppose, that I do have that precious integrity I was so eager to protect. I also have the ear of several big-shot media people, not to mention Lord Listowel and the various charities, so it really is down to me to make the most of my privileged position, both to develop my own career and to help and publicise the causes that mean so much to me.

I'd actually had a big opportunity, years before, to pursue the path of fame. When I was in my late twenties, in 1988, I had become the first personal trainer in the City of London. And in those days there was no such thing. There were gym instructors and boxing coaches, of course, but the special combination of skills and talents that makes a personal trainer had not been recognised.

As people started to become aware of this new type of trainer, there was a lot of misunderstanding about what we would do for our clients. More than one rich woman had got the impression that 'personal trainer' meant 'escort with muscles' and wanted the kind of workout money can't buy. That's not to say I wouldn't give it away, absolutely free of charge, to at least some of those who caught my eye and asked nicely. But that's pleasure, not business.

Once I'd got my reading and writing up to a standard where I could study properly, I'd taken a string of professional training courses to prepare me for working in a gym. Of course I needed to know the basics of anatomy and physiology, but I wanted to go a lot further than that. I took advanced courses and studied massage techniques and psychology, too, financing all this investment in myself with door work, body-guarding or providing security protection for the working girls in some of London's finest brothels.

My first break as a trainer came when I was offered a job at a very classy gym in the Barbican, right in the heart of the City. Every day I would find myself working with bankers and business tycoons, lawyers and media people. When the stars of Hollywood were in town, this was where they'd come, and I soon got used to rubbing shoulders with clients like Jodie Foster, Christopher Reeve and Charles Dance. As long as you were capable, discreet and professional, I found, these big name clients would take your advice and do what they were told. I had to sign non-disclosure agreements to protect their privacy, but they seemed to like my way of putting things across and I steadily became less star-struck and more confident that I had something to offer.

After a while, I began to build elements of boxing training into my aerobic workouts. This was something new at that time and it attracted a lot of attention. Clients wanted to try it and the media saw it as a new angle that made exercise sexy. The demand grew and grew, and I was perfectly positioned to make the most of it. Ordinary people can't be given the sort of demanding routines and ballistic stretching that I was used to in a boxing context, but I knew what ordinary health club members could safely tackle and I soon developed my own system of boxing-based training. It used familiar boxing training techniques like skipping, cardio blasts and pad work and I called it Boxerobics. When I started running classes at the Dance Works studio gym in Oxford Street, and then at other places around town, I quickly had more clients than I could handle.

Things started to move fast then, and I was contacted about devising some suitable boxing exercises for a fitness video that was about to be produced.

'It's going to be called *The Body Workout*,' they told me.

'Not a great name,' I thought. 'I wonder why they're calling it that.'

The answer soon became clear. The video was going to be made by the supermodel Elle 'The Body' Macpherson, generally recognised at that time as the woman with the world's most beautiful physique. To be fair, she's fifty now and still stunning, so that was hardly an exaggeration. We agreed terms and I worked on the exercise sequences in London before being flown out to Miami to help in shooting the pilot for the video. I never met Elle, as the final shoot was in New Zealand, but I was promised a place on the credits for the video that became one of the best-selling fitness DVDs of all time.

As it turned out, the credit never happened, but suddenly everyone seemed to know about my involvement and the press and television were all over me. I was interviewed in all the national papers and I was soon turning up on daytime television favourites like *The Big Breakfast* and on talk shows with people like Ross King and Anne and Nick.

Chris Evans and Paula Yates had me on *The Big Breakfast*

several times, demonstrating the sort of simple routines that people could do in their own homes. It worked well. Paula was a total professional, completely at home in front of the cameras, and she was very good at relaxing everyone else around her. When I froze up with first-day nerves, she waited until the red light was about to come on and then pinched my bum, hard, so I jumped a mile and fell about laughing. We spent time together before and after the shows and I got to meet an odd selection of celebrities, including Pierce Brosnan, Robin Williams, Julie Walters and Paula's then-secret lover, Michael Hutchence of INXS.

If I'd had a manager or an agent behind me – a business Svengali, a Simon Cowell or a Brian Epstein – I could have built a career off the back of all the media coverage. For a while, people did recognise me in the street. I was flavour of the month and there were all sorts of business, and other, opportunities coming at me from all directions. I've never been interested in drink or drugs. They're not my idea of the high life. But suddenly there were an amazing number of fantastic women who were keen to spend time with me. Fame is a powerful aphrodisiac, and I was too busy making the most of my good luck to worry about making my fortune.

Just recently I have been talking to a big TV company about a regular fitness show, which would cover the whole range, from sofa exercises for flabby couch potatoes to strenuous workouts with high-performance athletes and sportsmen. It's a good solid basis for a long-running show, but I should really have been doing it twenty years ago. I should have been cashing in on my television fame at the time and turning it into a business advantage that would last for years. But I missed my chance – partly because I didn't recognise the opportunity and partly because I didn't want to be a celebrity. I wanted to be a trainer. I couldn't see the obvious point that being a celebrity trainer, with regular exposure on television, was potentially something that could give me the best of both worlds.

My high profile was enough to attract a lot of attention to my trademarked Boxerobics system. The health and fitness editors at *Cosmopolitan* magazine had quickly spotted its appeal for their young and ambitious readers. Boxerobics shaped you up like nothing else did. It was fun and it was different. And it also gave women a chance to hit out a bit, to let off steam and work off their frustrations. *Cosmo* was often accused of being obsessed with sex, but it was only giving its readers what they wanted. For a certain sort of woman, Boxerobics seemed to stir the pheromones like nothing else. I wrote a column for *Cosmo* for several months and the magazine flew me all over the place, to all sorts of exotic locations in the States and Europe – half of them places I'd never even heard of.

But Boxerobics worked as a very enjoyable and efficient exercise system for men, too, and everyone wanted a piece of the magic. Trainers from all over London came to me for training and I could charge whatever I wanted to let them into the secrets of my method. Instead of twenty quid a session, I could get six times as much. Everything was building very nicely. But I took my eye off the ball.

All the time, while this flirtation with fame had been going on, I had carried on doing the rough, tough stuff at weekends, working on the doors with the same people I'd worked with for the last twelve years or so. I was still hard as nails and I was now very experienced as well. Often I could defuse situations simply because people could see I meant what I said. But sometimes, inevitably, the usual rough and tumble would get out of hand.

One night, I was running the door for a rather private little wine bar, just up the road from the pub that became the Sugar Hut, as featured on *TOWIE*. A favourite gathering place for some of the more serious faces on the Essex scene, it wasn't the sort of joint that welcomed passing strangers or bunches of happy drunks looking to go on somewhere after the pubs had shut, but there was rarely much trouble. I'd tell people, gently but firmly, that they should go elsewhere, and they usually did. The problem on this night was that the five well-oiled folk who turned up were friends of another, very inexperienced, doorman who was also working there. If he'd just told his mates their faces wouldn't fit, a lot of trouble might have been avoided.

As it was, after I'd told them politely that they weren't coming in, my colleague urged me to change my mind.

'Do me a favour,' he said. 'They're good guys and they won't be trouble. Trust me, I'll vouch for them.'

I'm usually stubborn. I'll back my own judgement and it takes a lot to make me change my mind. But this time I relented and let them in. And it only took a few minutes for me to start regretting it. As I said, there were some people in this wine bar you didn't want to mess with. So when the five outsiders started tossing lit cigarettes off the balcony onto the girls dancing below, shouting and laughing their heads off, I was worried someone might get murdered. I'd been called in when one of the staff had pressed the red panic button and I knew I had to get these big lumps out, fast, before the balloon went up. Already I could see some of the regulars exchanging meaningful looks.

'You're out,' I told the strangers. 'You've got to go. Believe me, you've got to get out of here.'

But I hadn't realised how drunk they were. This was getting urgent.

'Fuck off outside now.'

'Oh, yeah,' one hefty bloke said, stepping forward. 'Who's going to make us? You and whose army? There's five of us, pal, and just one of you.'

He was right that there was just me. Their friend, my fellow doorman, had disappeared. The backchat continued, but I was gradually able to manoeuvre all five of them towards the door and out onto the street. And that should have been the happy ending. Job done and no bones broken. It was no good me telling them that I'd probably saved them from a good hiding, maybe a cutting or worse. You get no thanks in this profession.

There were other punters queuing outside, of course, and we stood looking at each other under the lights, the five big oafs and me. I moved forward, off the step, to tell them to sober up and go home, and, at that moment, one of the ones at the side got brave and kicked my legs away from under me.

These are the street fighter's rules of the road.

Rule One – When you have to fight several opponents, keep moving so you're fighting one at a time. Isolate one, deal with him as quickly and thoroughly as possible, then pick out the next one.

Rule Two – Don't go down. Once you're on the floor, anything can happen. It's too easy. You can be dead or disabled in a matter of seconds. You can't get out of the way of anything and any fool can land a kick to your head, in the guts, in the nuts, anywhere. Get up or you're gone.

I was down, and the others all piled in straight away, jumping on me and kicking at my head. I couldn't get up, and I was being battered from all sides. I could hear my attackers laughing and shouting, and girls screaming in the queue a few yards away.

I must have been kicked twenty or thirty times, quite enough to rupture a spleen or cause brain damage if you're unlucky, when one of the other staff members came racing out and started pulling one or two of the geezers away from me. That was a distraction, and I scrambled to my feet and faced the gang of them.

Now it was fairer odds. My rescuer had taken a thump, so he was out of it, but now we were down to a straightforward five-to-one fight. With me on my feet, I was in with a chance. The guy who'd done all the talking came at me like a bullet and tried to headbutt me, but I ducked away and threw a big upper cut, dumping him on the floor with a mouth full of blood and teeth. His mate flew at me and I sidestepped him and slammed him against the glass door, which smashed and lacerated his arms and face. Any other time I'd have had some sympathy, but I was fighting for my life against the bloodlust of these five beered-up louts.

It must have been the sight of the guy who had gone through the door that unnerved the other three. They obviously didn't fancy it any more and so they legged it, just as the first two got it together to attack again. They'd both been badly hurt, as I had, so this was serious now and I think they wanted to kill me. I didn't want to kill anyone, but I wanted to be sure they wouldn't keep coming back at me. When they came for me, I hit them again and again, heavy, crunching blows, until first one and then the other collapsed in a bloodied heap on the ground.

I was still standing there in my blood-soaked tuxedo, blood streaming from cuts to my head and somebody's teeth embedded in the knuckles of my left fist, when the police arrived. They took a lot of photographs, impounded the tapes from the CCTV cameras and charged me, there and then, with Grievous Bodily Harm and the even more serious charge of GBH with intent.

It didn't look good. Three of the five goons who'd attacked me and kicked me when I was on the pavement had gone, so it was hard for me to explain how close I had come to being the one and only victim of this vicious battle. I was the last man standing, so I had to have been the bully.

I was still going out with Anthea at the time and she came with me to Brentwood police station. You could see her fellow cops didn't approve.

'Don't you know what that guy does for a living?' they asked her.

As far as they were concerned, I was just a bouncer, a thug. They didn't know I was one of London's hottest personal trainers and the man behind the success of Boxerobics – and they wouldn't have given a toss, anyway. Standing there in a police cell in a white shirt spattered with blood, I was once again that troubled kid from St

Leonard's. Was Coral going to be right, after all this time?

I can't help dwelling on things. There's always been the feeling that deep down I'm not worthy. Maybe what the coppers in the police station thought they saw was what I really was. My friends are always telling me off for saying 'With my luck…' and I always expect the worst, though actually my luck is usually pretty good. That night, I felt my luck had run out.

It was 18 months before the case came to trial. In the run-up, I had to report regularly to the magistrates court and I also had to go and get permission from the police before I could leave the country. Meanwhile my personal training work was booming and it was taking me abroad again and again, with trips to America and the Caribbean and all over Europe. That meant I kept on having to go to the police station, so I was always being reminded of the trouble I was in and the prison sentence that seemed almost certain to follow the trial. I felt I was on borrowed time.

Because the training was going so well, I had a tremendous opportunity. If circumstances had been different, I would have been able to make the most of the international contacts I was making, the personal referrals from big name stars and the exposure I'd been getting on television and in the press. As it was, I found it hard enough just to keep going. Most nights I had nightmares, and they didn't go away during the day. I worked ridiculous hours, trying to keep my mind off the trial that lay ahead and trying not to remember Auntie Coral's menacing prediction that I'd end up in a prison cell. But I simply wasn't in the right frame of mind to turn being slightly famous into a long-term career as a TV fitness guru.

That was how I missed the boat, when fame lay at my feet. By the time my case came up, I was worn to a shadow and fearing the worst. GBH with intent could get me five years in jail. Even my own barrister suggested I should plead guilty to the lesser charge of GBH, as that would mean a shorter sentence.

I wasn't going to do that, though. Why should I? I'd been fighting for my life to defend myself against a bunch of drunken and very aggressive hoodlums and I truly felt I had done nothing wrong. There was one witness who gave evidence that the five men had attacked me first, but no one else from the queue was prepared to appear in court. Without more witnesses, I didn't have a lot of faith that the truth would set me free, but I wasn't going to plead guilty.

For once, I got lucky. Another jury might have seen everything very differently. These guys listened hard, weighed up the evidence on both sides and made up their own minds.

The unanimous verdict – Not Guilty on both charges, on the grounds that reasonable force was used – came as a surprise to me and almost everyone in the court. The jury had basically decided that it had been them or me, and that I'd done what I needed to survive. I'd been right to think I was in imminent danger. My violence had to exceed theirs, because otherwise I was at serious risk of being killed. I was free to go, and the judge commented that the prosecution should never have gone ahead. 'A waste of taxpayers' money,' he called it.

Looking back, I know that case and all the tensions around it changed me. I gave up security work and focused on steadily building up my career as a personal trainer. For a while, I felt it had knocked the stuffing out of me. I wanted a quiet life and I didn't have the energy and ambition to follow up all the opportunities that had come my way. Gradually, the phone stopped ringing with offers of interviews and TV appearances. The moment had passed. It was not until my book came out, many years later, in 2010, that I saw the bright lights of a television studio again and experienced once more the strange sensation of walking down a street full of strangers, where half the people that pass by know who you are.

CHAPTER 19

ENDOCARDITIS? WHAT'S THAT?

As I gradually woke up and became aware of my surroundings, I could see two men standing near the foot of my bed. At first I couldn't make out where I was or what was going on, but I could hear them talking in hushed tones.

'What's it at now?' asked one.

'Seventy per cent,' said the other. 'Not good.'

'What do you think?'

'Better have a word with the patient's wife, I suppose. She may want to bring the children in. I don't know if they're religious, but she might want to get hold of a priest.'

The two doctors moved away and I tried to make sense of the situation. I was in hospital, obviously. And it sounded serious. I was pretty confused, and they told me later that I had been delirious, mumbling and shouting out a lot of stuff that wouldn't have been fit for a daytime audience. Now I felt like shit, but I was awake enough to know that things must be bad if they were talking about fetching the kids and calling in a priest.

I'd been brought in to Basildon University Hospital by ambulance, arriving just as Jo was leaving the building. Her nan had just died and she had gone there to pay her respects. So she got the shock of her life when she saw me being wheeled in just as she came out. She knew I'd been sick, suffering feverish flu-like symptoms and losing weight alarmingly, but neither of us had thought I'd end up being rushed in as an emergency.

I'd been trying to tough it out, to keep on working. When you're self-employed the money stops when you do. Getting ill's a luxury. So I'd been plugging on, working up to eighty hours a week, training some forty personal clients, filming my successful weight-loss programme for Channel 4's *Who Knows Best?* as well as writing my book. Normally I have to eat something like 5,000 calories a day, just to keep going – roughly twice the average male calorie intake – and all that extra stuff was burning even more calories. I should have been starving. But I'd been off my food and the weight had been dropping off me, leaving me looking awful and feeling worse. I'd had a fever that came and went, and I kept breaking out in violent hot and cold sweats, night after night. I'd been to talk to the doctor, but no one could figure out what was wrong.

When I'd gone back to the GP again, he'd taken one look at me, listened to my heart and called the ambulance.

The news was just as bad as it could be. I was suffering from something called infective endocarditis, the result of a leaky heart valve and a raging infection that had spread through my body from a tooth that had become diseased. This was serious. My heart was enlarged and I wasn't just ill. I was at death's door.

When endocarditis gets a grip like that, people don't usually come through it. The doctors took Jo to one side and explained that I'd be lucky to survive another twenty-four hours.

'I'm sorry, Mrs Connolly,' one said. 'We're doing everything we can, but I'm afraid he probably isn't going to make it through the night.'

The doctors suggested she should fetch the boys and bring them in to say goodbye to me. If she wanted me to be given the Last Rites, she should tell the priest to be quick.

I don't know how long Jo was gone. I was still lying there, burning up with the fever, feeling like death, waiting for her to come back, when a tall, gentle black man appeared at my side and took my hands in his. I've got small, rather delicate hands and I've always been a bit self-conscious about them. His were huge, broad and strong. Because I was so hot, they felt cold as ice. I had no idea who the tall man was, but the cool firmness of his hands was very calming.

'I just want to say a few words,' he said. 'I can give you some comfort, if you'll let me.'

I was too delirious to understand what was going on, but he spoke to me quietly, comfortingly, and I started to feel a bit stronger.

I didn't know too much about it at the time, but I realised later that he must have been the priest. The weird thing was, though, no one else had seen him. No one had been seen going into my ward. No one had come out. Yet I'd had this visitor who'd somehow made me feel better. And no one, Jo told me later, had been called to give the Last Rites.

Despite the doctors' fears, I was still alive the next morning. After a couple of days, they told Jo I was stable and that it looked like I was going to make it. My very high level of overall fitness had helped my body fight back. The sepsis was responding to the antibiotic drip, and I was over the worst.

But in all the weeks I spent in that place, I never saw the man who had comforted me again, and no one could ever tell me who he was.

★ ★ ★

As I started to get better, I began to worry about how my boys were reacting to my illness. Archie was too young to understand, but Harley had been very upset because he knew I was desperately sick and might be going to die. Little Archie kept trying to dive-bomb the bed but I didn't have the energy to stop him. I felt weak as a baby, like I'd been run over by a truck.

That wasn't good, and as soon as I really began to feel I was on my way back, I had to do something about it. I had lost strength and muscle mass and I worried that I wouldn't even be able to work when I got back home. The doctors told me I'd probably be in hospital for three months and I knew that would leave me in a terrible state. So I started slipping out into the stairwell and doing some light training. It wasn't a great idea, I suppose. I couldn't stop myself, though. Exercise has always been the one thing that makes me feel good. There I was, like an idiot, doing quick sprints up and down the staircases, carrying my drip bottle, and doing press-ups between floors.

The doctors were alarmed.

'Is this really necessary, Paul?' one of them asked. 'You've almost died. What you should be doing now is having a good long rest.'

He didn't know — how could he? — what life is like for me. I can't help it. It's rooted deep in my background. Feeling that I'm doing my best to stay fit and strong really is a matter of life and death for me. When I feel weak, I feel I might as well be dead.

In the end, I spent one month in the hospital. I was a caged tiger and my old demons were back with a vengeance. Never mind my health, I was telling myself that I'd never be able to work again, I couldn't pay the bills and everything would fall to pieces. I was focusing on the negative stuff and having nightmares about what might happen to my family. I was champing at the bit, and I couldn't wait to get out. I'd look forward to the training in the stairwell, but apart from that — and some of the doctors were dead set against it — the main thing I looked forward to was visits from friends.

My mates had done everything they could to make things go well for me. Before I'd even come round from the operation, Ian had persuaded the staff to move my bed to a quiet corner by the window. He knew I'd never relax and recover if I felt jumpy and exposed in the middle of a busy ward, with staff and visitors coming and going either side of me. I thought I just happened to get lucky and get the corner bed, but it wasn't like that.

James, from Fitness First, had come in carrying an innocent-looking Tesco bag. When no one was watching, he leaned across to me.

'I thought you might like these,' he whispered. 'Better put them somewhere where people won't see them. They might object.'

I looked in the bag. Good old James! A pair of dumbbells. Just what every hospital patient needs.

As I got stronger, my visitors would take me down to the hospital restaurant to get a proper meal. The normal hospital food was mainly awful cheap microwave meals – chemicals on a plate – so it was a relief when I could slip off downstairs with my mates and tuck into a pie and chips.

Visiting hours were flexible and one morning my dapper friend Chris Clapshaw came in to have breakfast in the ward with me. He's a thoughtful guy and an old buddy, through good times and bad. During the nightmare of my week-long trial on GBH charges, in the mid-nineties, Chris would turn up in court, day after day, to give me moral support and, eventually, to cheer when the jury found me Not Guilty. Now he came along, impeccably dressed as always, to brighten up my breakfast.

We were just getting started when a voice came from the next bed.

'Excuse me,' the old boy lying there broke in. 'But could you get me a bedpan?'

I found him a bedpan and closed the curtains around his bed so he could use it.

'My God,' said Chris. 'The old codger's not going to do a piss right next to you, while you're eating, is he?'

But I was used to it by then.

'It's a hospital,' I said, picking up my toast. 'We're all in it together.'

We got on with our breakfast and tried to ignore what was going on next door. But you couldn't ignore it for long. My unhappy neighbour missed, and moments later the urine was trickling round my bed. Chris looked horrified.

'Don't worry,' I said. 'Someone will be along to clean it up.'

'But it's urine, all over the floor!'

'Come on, eat your breakfast. Piss is sterile. Forget about it.'

The sound of wind filled the ward and the stench of shit wafted towards us as the eighty-year-old relieved himself into his bedpan.

'Sorry, Paul,' said Chris, turning pale and visibly gagging. 'Got to go. I can't do this. I'm afraid I'm going to be sick!'

He fled the scene, while the nurses and I just fell about in hysterics at the sight of his retreating back. Chris is so posh, so polite, such a gentleman. I laughed till it hurt, till I was gasping for breath. I'd never have guessed he could run that fast. I got on with my breakfast and the poor old bastard in the next-door bed died a couple of days later, after vomiting blood for several hours.

As I got better, I started to think about my business and about the non-stop job of promoting my book. I ended up being interviewed in my hospital bed by three of the local papers and my old friends at BBC Radio Essex. I even had a meeting in the hospital with a guy from a film production company. His firm had heard that *Against All Odds* was about to be published and wanted to talk about making a movie of it. Names like Jason Statham and Bruce Willis were being bandied about, but I notice neither of them has called yet for my advice on how to portray me. Maybe I should check my phone charger.

In between these flurries of activity, visits from friends and family and increasingly energetic exercise sessions on the hospital staircases were the only highlights that kept me sane. Little things came to mean a lot. I'd made friends with The Colonel, an Essex scrap dealer who'd just had some painful surgery, and we were delighted when we discovered a private toilet that nobody ever seemed to use. We nicked the key that was in the door and had exclusive access to this personal convenience for the rest of my month in the hospital.

There was no getting away from the fact that it felt like serving time. I've never been to prison, though once or twice I've come close. But being in hospital obviously has some similarities. For example, I had a hell of a lot of time to think.

One thing I kept coming back to was the way my past has never quite left me. I had been in hospital, close to death, because of a combination of a weakened heart and an infection in my mouth. The problem had been festering behind dental work I'd had done after some teeth were knocked out with a baseball bat when I was working as a doorman in my twenties. My teeth have always been bad because of the poor nutrition I received at St Leonard's – and the years of brawling and fisticuffs afterwards can't have helped.

Like all the kids in the home, I grew up malnourished, surviving mainly on white bread and jam, and not nearly enough of it. I'm only average height, and when I look at the size of my own kids I can see I was probably meant to be a lot taller. Harley is already tall for his age, and four-year-old Archie must be well on his way towards playing rugby for England.

The children in the home were not taken to the dentist on any kind of regular basis, because dentists cost money. Together with the atrocious diet, this meant that almost all of us had terrible teeth. Once in a while, someone had a bad tooth pulled out, but that was as far as it went. I didn't go to the dentist till I was in my twenties, by which stage my teeth were so bad I got a right telling-off. I'd had to teach myself about oral hygiene and diet, but most of the damage had already been done when I was a child. The dental problem that landed me in intensive care had had its roots back in my childhood.

While I'm hugely grateful to the NHS for taking care of me and patching me up, the economics of things like this make no sense at all. I was in hospital for a month, and my care will have cost nearly £50,000. For the sake of a few quid saved on dental fees forty years ago, I got sick and had to be treated at the state's expense. As financial planning goes, that's just crap.

But my hospital musings weren't all about economics. I also thought a lot about my own life and my own future. Why did I become ill?

There were clear physical reasons for the problem, but I do think the stress that bubbled up in the course of writing my book and doing all the media interviews had a lot to do with it. I'd kept so many memories and feelings suppressed for years, and I reckon it was just a matter of time before they reared up again. They came out through my weak points – the awful teeth that are the legacy of my childhood and the damaged heart that had managed to keep going all those years. I'd been working too hard, like I always did, and perhaps that didn't help. But hard work never hurt me before. I believe the illness was a wake-up call that told me I needed to get to grips with my emotional and spiritual wellbeing, as well as my physical health.

CHAPTER 20

WHAT'S INSIDE

After I'd been rushed to hospital and come so close to dying, yet again, I became terrified that something was going to happen to me. Next time, I was sure, I wouldn't be so lucky.

It wasn't myself I was worried about. Having my first child had changed everything. I had spent my life trying to survive. I'd been alone in the world, in and out of jobs, relationships and situations, just trying to stay afloat, to keep going and make everything work. I carried the scars of my childhood with me everywhere I went, but gradually I'd started to build a career. Gradually, too, from the time I met Jo, I'd started to build a life that had room for someone else alongside me. But it was Harley's birth, nearly ten years ago, that truly gave me a purpose.

From the moment this tiny, perfect baby came into the world, I knew I had something to live for. I had someone who needed my strength and my tenderness, loved me unconditionally and depended on me for a start in life that would be very different from my own.

We called him Harley at my insistence. I never explained why, but Jo thought it suited him, so Harley he became. It was only years later, when he was about four, that she discovered why I'd wanted that name for my firstborn son.

He was playing outside in the garden and Jo was busy cooking in the kitchen, under the signed photo of my hero, Cassius Clay, that hangs on the wall. I don't remember what I was doing, but I wanted to speak to the boy about something, so I shouted to him to come in.

'Oi, 'Arley,' I called. 'Leave that and come in 'ere a minute!'

Suddenly Jo was right in my face, with a strange look I'd never seen before.

'Paul,' she said. 'You didn't?'

'Didn't what?'

'You didn't call our son Harley just so that every time you spoke his name it would sound like Ali, did you?'

It didn't matter. She'd liked the name, too, or he'd have been called something different. But yes, that might have had something to do with it. My Essex accent is a part of me that's never going to change, so there are never going to be many 'H' sounds at the beginning of my words. And Muhammad Ali, for me, represents everything I'd hope my son would grow up to be – strong, gracious, big-hearted, intelligent, determined and generous.

I thought Jo might be cross, but she just stood there looking at me with such love and understanding that I knew it would be all right.

'Yeah, I s'ppose I did. You don't mind, do you?'

'Course not, you idiot! It's a lovely name. And it's even better now I know what it means to you.'

Now that's what I call a wife and mother.

'I love you, Paul. And I love how you love him. But I hope you haven't got plans like that for this next one.' She stroked her bump. 'This one's going to be called Archie.'

Since Harley and Archie came into my life, being there for my children has been the most important thing in the world for me. Being a father gave me strength and purpose. But it also made me vulnerable in new ways.

As soon as I got home after my month in hospital, I went back to work. The doctors had expected me to spend ninety days convalescing, but I took my first fitness sessions just three days after getting back. I was worried about money and I couldn't afford to let things go for weeks or months. During all the life-and-death drama of my illness, my best mate, Ian, had made sure the wheels didn't come off. He'd been an absolute star. He'd quietly paid the bills, kept a float of a couple of grand in my bank account at all times and helped Jo out in all sorts of ways. He'd been amazing, but there was no way I could let him continue carrying us. Not working, even for the first few weeks while I got my strength back, simply wasn't an option.

It was as I started to build up again towards full fitness that I noticed something else had changed. This time the brush with death had scared me rigid and I was beginning to worry a lot about illness. I started thinking I was coming down with something awful every time I felt a twinge or ache, until I was getting on for being a full-blown hypochondriac. My OCD tendencies, never far below the surface, bubbled up in ways that couldn't be ignored. I started having panic attacks, and my GP put me on anti-depressants. Medically, it probably seemed like a sensible decision. But the drugs made me feel weak and useless – and that's pretty depressing.

The anxieties I'd always struggled to control began to haunt me. I was becoming possessive and overprotective. I'd always been a fan of American sports, but that wasn't enough to explain the unusual number of baseball bats in various places around the house, as a result of my constant worries about people breaking in and threatening my family. I never wanted to be in a position of not being able to defend myself or my loved ones. But, of course, baseball bats and knuckledusters are no bloody good when it comes to keeping illness at bay and the endocarditis scare had left me poorly equipped, psychologically, to keep my dreads and demons under control.

For all those years, after I'd left the children's home and started to build a life of my own, I'd had nothing to lose. I would get into fights without a second thought, for good reasons, bad reasons or no reasons at all. I was hurt, angry, strong, unstoppable. I'd been beaten and burnt and battered around from the age of eight. I knew pain, and I wasn't afraid of it – not of copping it myself, nor of dishing it out.

At times, I think I even enjoyed being hurt. It made you feel alive, like something real was going on. And I certainly got a lot of pleasure from inflicting pain on others.

I'd rationalise it, of course. It was them or me, I'd think. Some mouthy fucker had caused trouble and needed to be taken down a peg. I saw myself as the Lone Ranger, the righter of wrongs, society's unofficial policeman. Where the law left off, I'd take over.

If someone was driving badly and cut in on me, it was time they were taught a lesson. I believed in adult education. I'd drag the other driver from his car and humiliate him. If he showed any sign at all of wanting a fight, I'd punch the shit out of him. I was road rage waiting to happen.

If someone said the wrong thing to a girl I was with, or tried to force their way in when I was working as doorman at a club, they'd be in danger of getting a beating they'd never forget. But it wasn't just blood and bruises, I'd leave some of those bastards with scars they'd keep for the rest of their lives. It was violent, disproportionate, almost unhinged. But it made me feel better. In some warped way, I was getting back at the world that had done me down, hitting back at Bill Starling and the loathsome Auntie Coral.

Looking back on it, I shudder. Nothing I did in those years had any impact whatsoever on Starling, Coral or Prescott – the people I might justifiably have wanted to hurt or kill. Flailing about, I was insane with rage against them and the society that had let them treat us kids the way they did. Some of those I hit really deserved to be clumped. Mostly, though, the people who got hurt were the relatively innocent bystanders, the tipsy bigmouths who ought to have been shooed off home and the careless or pushy drivers who cut me up. Someone told me these days you can be fined in Germany just for flashing a V-sign or a finger at another road user. In my part of the world, at that time, there were no fines, but the punishments were swift and terrible.

And I always came out on top. Partly, it was because I was a boxer, trained to hit, to defend myself, to take blows and to win. I'd learned from Muhammad Ali's wisdom. He knew. Always it was there in the back of my mind: 'Nothing wrong with going down... It's staying down that's wrong.'

In the early days after the children's home, I believed I had a future. My boxing was going great. I was hard, skilful and unafraid. The coaches at Dagenham Boxing Club had become my mentors and almost my guardians while I was going through the later years at St Leonard's. Besides teaching me a lot about boxing, they'd kept an eye out for me in other ways. They'd feed me when they could see I was hungry. They'd pick me up to take me to fights, as I worked my way up through the amateur rankings. In my small, closed-off world, they were the only adults who treated me with respect and warmth, without some ulterior motive and agenda of their own. They could see I had talent and the hunger to win, along with a willingness to train and learn and push myself until it hurt. With their help and a long series of wins under my belt – both in the ring and in the ugly, messy street fights I was always getting into – I came to believe I could handle any physical challenge life threw at me.

Later, of course, the sudden, devastating impact of my fall from the roof and the injuries to my arm and hand snatched away my hopes of a boxing career. But although it took me two years to get right again, the accident hadn't really had a long-term effect on my physical courage or confidence.

I still believed I could look after myself in any situation. Through the years that followed, I still did security work in some very difficult places, still risked my neck and still got away with it, time and again. I was still the man with nothing to lose, and that made me unbeatable. Besides I had a well-earned reputation for never giving up. If someone wanted to stop me, they'd have to kill me.

But that all changed when first Jo and then the boys came into my life. They needed me. Now I had something to protect and something to lose, and it took away that steely edge I'd had. I was Samson with a haircut. Sometimes I was Samson with a headache. To be fair, I'd given up getting into fights or working the doors a couple of years earlier, in the late 1990s, after coming within an ace of being sent down on those charges of Grievous Bodily Harm and GBH with intent. That shook me rigid. If it hadn't been for a realistic jury deciding that I'd used reasonable force against the five people who attacked me, I'd have been facing at least five years in prison.

So I'd packed it all in and concentrated hard on the day job, the personal training. There'd been just one more major violent incident in my life, on Millennium Night, when I'd unwisely come out of retirement to do some door work to help out an old friend. I wasn't keen, but it was a grand in the hand – and a thousand quid for a night's work makes it hard to say no.

Needless to say, it had all gone tits up. Everyone was overexcited and everything got overheated. Worse, the other people on the door were bloody amateurs and walked off just when I was trying to sort out two ugly customers we had thrown out. They both turned on me and things got nasty, especially when one of the bastards bit a lump out of my chest. I have a fine collection of scars, here, there and everywhere, but that bite-shaped exhibit is one of strangest. I went berserk and nearly killed the pair of them, pounding away till one had a broken jaw and both were on their knees in the car park. I was more Mike Tyson than Muhammad Ali that night, and I frightened myself.

I had a tetanus jab for the bite on my chest, and some wag at the hospital offered me rabies, too, but I declined, as the guy hadn't actually been foaming at the mouth. Still, the whole thing had been frightening. Once I got started, I could easily have killed those two idiots. I was lucky I didn't.

I decided that really was the end for violence and me, except in the strictest self-defence. Fourteen years on, I have come close a few times, but I've been, as we say, violence-free. It's a bit like alcoholism – one day at a time is the only way you can do it. And, believe me, sometimes it's hard.

The urge to hit out is often there, just below the veneer of calm respectability, but I have to rein it in. Jo detests violence, so I have to be non-violent if I'm going to be the man I want to be for her. Kids grow up to imitate what they see around them and I don't want Harley and Archie learning that stuff from me. I feel the strain, as well as the pleasure, of being their role model. There must be no more fights.

But fighting the invisible, potentially deadly attack from the endocarditis was something different. It made me feel mortal, vulnerable. I hated the fact that I could do nothing to defend myself, and it planted fears and uncertainties inside me, just when I wanted to be strong and protective towards my growing family.

Worse still, I began to fear the ghosts of my past. I began believing my physical illness was triggered – or at least somehow helped – by all the poisonous shit still bubbling around inside me, left over from my childhood. It felt as if it just needed to find a chink in my armour, any slight physical or mental weakness, to be on me and causing serious trouble.

The doctors told me I'd been born with a leaky heart valve, but I couldn't help feeling there was a psychosomatic side to my illness. It didn't seem likely that stress and anxiety could cause an infection deep inside me, but they won't have helped my immune system fight back. It seemed I could fight all I wanted, but my past was always there, lurking like a dark shadow.

It was my friend Ian who eventually had the love and courage to warn me I was getting close to the edge.

'You've trained your body all your life, mate, but that's not what you need now,' he said. 'You haven't trained your mind. Maybe it's time to start looking at doing a bit of mental training for a change.'

That threw up some weird images, but I knew what he meant. There's a sign on the wall at our gym that says 'A strong mind starts with a fit body' and I've always believed that. But even having a superfit trainer's body wasn't necessarily going to be enough, on its own, to help me through.

Looking back, maybe it was a mistake to do the book and all the interviews and events that followed its launch without a bit of mental support in handling the emotions it all stirred up. It might have been a smart move to book some therapy sessions. But my past experience of shrinks and therapists had been very mixed, so I wasn't so sure it would help. Now that even my best mate was getting alarmed at my mental state, it was time to take a chance on finding the right kind of approach to tackle the problem.

I'm not a therapist's dream. I've got a lot locked away inside me and I don't find it easy to get things out. To be fair, I'm also a bit resistant, slightly sceptical. So I was lucky when a friend put me in touch with a great organisation known as Thrive and I met a counsellor of theirs called Alice.

Thrive's aim is to teach people practical ways to change their attitudes. It's all about focusing on the positives in your situation and not looking only at the negatives. But it's not just a question of singing 'Always Look on the Bright Side of Life' all day and every day.

Alice was able to help by teaching me new techniques and strategies and ways of looking at myself and the events around me. She didn't like the way I talked to myself. As she pointed out, I spent a lot of my time saying negative things, like 'God, I'm such a fucking idiot! That's so typical!' or 'Bloody hell, here I go again!', effectively training my mind to be tuned in to the negative aspects of life. Think like that and everything that happens seems to confirm your own stupidity and makes it hard to focus on the positive things you experience and the positive qualities in yourself.

Thrive teaches you how to reframe this negative chatter inside and notice the positive stuff. Alice gave me a great slogan, 'Fake it till you make it', that helps with this. I love that. It recognises that you're in the habit of thinking negatively and that changing that is hard. So you just say to yourself, 'How would I see this situation now, *if* I could see it in a positive way?' It helps to integrate positive thinking into the way you look at the world, and that made it a very useful little tool for me.

I discovered that whenever bad things happened, I'd always pushed them aside and got on with life the best way I knew how. Alice helped me realise that, as I'm getting older, I must finally rid myself of the psychological demons that have been tormenting me for years, or they will kill me. They had already come damn close.

Suddenly it was clear that I was my own worst enemy. Other people weren't nearly as nasty to me as I was to myself. I needed to learn the difference between what's real and what isn't, what can be changed and what can't. And that's not all that easy. We all get stressed about things that happened a long time ago, or that happened a certain way and might have been different. I did it obsessively, and it did me no good. It made me think like a victim – and if you think like a victim, you become one. I needed Thrive's shot of positivity and it came to me at just the right time.

I started learning how to change negative thought patterns into positive ones and how to speak more nicely to myself. This was a journey I had to take on my own. Jo is a wonderful support, but she has her hands full with the kids – and no matter how well she knows and loves me, she can't get inside my head and feel things the way I do. Nobody can, and I wouldn't want her to try. My issues belong to me and they're a burden no one else should have to carry. Ultimately, my emotional problems are something I must deal with on my own.

Strangely, it's been harder to stay positive as I've grown older, even though my life is better now in almost every way. When I was young I always had a blind faith that things would work out for me, even when the evidence suggested the opposite and despite all the wrong decisions I took. Now I'm a happily settled dad, maybe on some level I worry that it's all going to be taken away from me because I don't deserve it. I needed Thrive's help to start training my mind to be positive, to see the good in life and believe it was meant for me, too.

So I got a lot out of it and I'm grateful to Alice and Rob Kelly, Thrive's founder. I've done some public speaking gigs since then in connection with Thrive, and I spoke at their annual convention and got a great reception – a standing ovation, actually – from the big audience of therapists and psychologists. They were very interested in the mental and emotional abuse the St Leonard's kids had been put through, as well as the sexual abuse and physical beatings.

It's funny how little sticks when you do therapy and courses. You can spend hours focused on something, picking it apart and concentrating very hard. And what are you left with a few months later? A slight change of attitude, maybe, and a few extra resources you can use when times are rough. But, for me, that one slogan has been worth its weight in gold: 'Fake it till you make it'.

I think I'd always felt I was faking it and that I didn't deserve any of the good things that happened to me. Worse, I noticed the bad things and thought, 'Quite right, too.' Now I'm looking for positives and the world looks different.

I had a shitty childhood. It's in there, and it's part of what I am. I was a fucked-up kid and a pretty damaged young adult. Yet having that story to tell has given me something to give to the world. I told the bare bones of it in *Against All Odds* and it made me a best-selling author. My problems with illiteracy have helped Beanstalk recruit new volunteers to help more of today's kids before reading becomes a problem for them, too. And my own history helps me get through to the troubled boys at the Ramsden Hall school. My abusive care home experience is helping campaigners like Lord Listowel publicise the need for reform, even now, to improve things for a new generation of underprivileged kids. Looked at the right way, it's all good.

Those Monty Python guys were no fools. No fools at all.

'Always look on the bright side of life, de dum, de dum de dum de dum...'

CHAPTER 21

FAQs

These days I'm a trainer. And a massage therapist. And a survivor of St Leonard's. I'm an author who couldn't write till he was in his late twenties and a motivational speaker. I'm a businessman, a father, and a husband. I'm an ex-boxer, an ex-bouncer and a campaigner for better care homes and more help for kids who can't read.

When I find myself up in front of an audience, I never know what I'm going to be asked about. So here's a random selection of the questions I get thrown at me, and some answers on topics ranging from Hollywood and what it's like to be stabbed to why 'fat skinny birds' need to build up muscle density.

What do the local people feel about St Leonard's now?
To be honest, a lot of them still aren't aware of what was going on there in the past. The old buildings along The Drive stood derelict for several years after the home was

closed down in the mid-eighties, gradually deteriorating as local recycling enthusiasts with a head for heights climbed up and stripped the lead from its roofs. It did give a boost to the local economy, though, as those of us who were in the roofing trade and used a lot of lead were able to give very competitive quotes for a year or two.

The cottages were eventually split up and converted into nice luxury homes that now sell at £600,000 a go. When we were young, everyone – children and carers alike – believed the cottages were haunted. But none of the new residents, as far as I'm aware, have been bothered by ghosts, either from the Victorian era or from our troubled time there.

When they did the redevelopment, the story of the abuse at the home still hadn't broken, so one of the roads was named Prescott Way. I remembered Prescott's ways, so I was horrified. Once the facts started to come out, the road was renamed pretty promptly. No one really wanted to live in a road named after a convicted paedophile.

As recently as 2012, the builders Bellway were developing a site a few yards down the road and they thought they'd give the new place a touch of class by coming up with a posh name. They chose 'St Leonard's Hamlet', and people in Hornchurch were, quite rightly, up in arms. We had a campaign and I joined in with a couple of local activists, Lorraine Moss and Councillor Barbara Matthews, to do press interviews and bring pressure on Bellway to think again. In all fairness, the developers just hadn't known the history and the evil connotations of the St Leonard's name and they changed it as soon as we told them the background.

There are lots of friends and relatives of the kids who suffered at the home who still live round these parts. They'd have hated to be reminded of it all, day in and day out, so it was definitely the right decision. As for the people living in the converted buildings, I know a few of them and they've carefully avoided reading my first book, *Against All Odds*. I understand that. They don't want to know. If they really understood what had gone on within those walls, they'd probably want to move out straight away.

As a former boxer, what do you think about cage fighting?
It's interesting. I train cage fighters. I've had two or three cage fighters that have come to me for training with their boxing. One of them is Neil 'Goliath' Grove and we've done a little video clip together that you can find on YouTube. Neil's a really big bloke, a 6-foot-4-inch South African, a British champion and a nice guy. He's among the top fighters in America now.

Cage fighting is mixed martial arts and those guys all come from different backgrounds, from wrestling and taekwondo to sumo and jiu jitsu, so they are usually great grapplers and wrestlers and throwers. But not many of them were boxers, so they tend to be weaker at striking. A lot of them come to boxing coaches to learn to punch more effectively. But you can't slip a punch and drop inside in a cage fight, because you're going to find a knee meets you in the face. I'm able to help people like Neil with their balance and boxing technique, giving them advantages like an extra inch or two on their jab, which could make all the difference in a fight.

Cage fighting is very technical and I don't think it will

ever be as popular as boxing, because boxing has such traditions, but it attracts massive audiences now, around the world. I still prefer boxing, though, because I don't know enough about what's happening on the floor, with all the wrestling and grappling, to make it interesting for me.

When I watch boxing, I'm watching for all sorts of different skills. I'm watching fighters swaying inside punches and using ringcraft. I'm watching them slipping guys and using the ropes, and using their brains, too. I'm watching for good boxers who know how to in-fight and turn their fights around. It's footwork and ringcraft and how to slip and duck and how to hit without being hit. To me, that's the Noble Art. That's our history. That's where we come from, right the way back to the Lonsdale Belt and the Queensberry Rules of 1867.

How bad was your reading when you left St Leonard's at nearly eighteen?
It was non-existent – I couldn't read or write at all. I could read my name, because I'd seen it written down so many times. If I'd tried to, I could have written my name. But pens and paper, forms and notes, they just weren't part of my life. I just got by without them.

I'm a positive person, so I tried to make out it wasn't an issue. I'd have told you I didn't need it, though I obviously did. But I was still sure I was going to be a professional boxer, so I really thought I'd pay someone to do that for me.

Why can't you name names about the Hollywood stars you trained?
You don't mess with these people. When you're going to

work with the top film stars, you have to sign strict confidentiality agreements. I remember I was doing some work at the VIP gym in Hollywood, in the Marina del Rey area, and there were lots of celebrities around and I was obviously going to be working on some world-famous bodies. The confidentiality agreements take the form of long, long contract documents and I was in an office and they put this big fat book down on the desk in front of me.

'Sign it,' they told me.

'I will,' I said. 'But I'm going to read it first.'

'No, you're not,' they said. 'You're not going to read it. You're just going to sign it.'

You work on their terms, or not at all. Basically, you could sum up the contract as saying everything is forbidden and you agree to that. It says, in formal legal language, 'If you, the undersigned, so much as breathe a word about us to anybody, now or in the future, we'll sue your arse from here to China and use your testicles as paperweights.' I may not have the wording quite right, but it's something like that. 'You see if we don't.'

I can talk about working on the *Body Workout* video for Elle Macpherson, because the people involved in that stitched me up by failing to give me the promised credit on the best-selling DVD. That's a major breach of contract and I could sue them for that. If anyone came out of the woodwork and said I shouldn't mention that Elle Macpherson connection, I would be very happy to sue them for the loss I took by not having my name on it. I've got all the contracts and paperwork, so there wouldn't be much argument about it.

There's a funny story here, though. The production company I did the work for was called Pickwick Pictures and they let me down badly by not putting my credit on the DVD. Years later, they came back to me and said, 'Can you do a load of new stuff for us?' Well, I'm not a fool. So I said, 'Not likely. I'm not working for you arseholes again. You screwed me.'

'Oh no,' they said. 'We would never do that. It's not the same company now. Everyone's left. We're all new. We're different people.'

So I did another load of work for them, and they did me over again. They screwed me again. It doesn't always work to believe the best in people.

Do you have one piece of advice for people doing running as part of their exercise routine?
Don't go on the same route, at the same time of day, over and over again. I'm serious. It's a simple safety precaution, but it's important.

I know of a girl who was attacked because she made the mistake of running the same route, at the same time, past the same flats, every day. They dragged her into the flats and raped her.

But it's easy to get into a habit. Jo used to always do her same favourite run at the same time until I told her she really must change it every day or two.

What does it feel like to be stabbed?
That depends on what you're stabbed with. I was stabbed with a Stanley knife and you don't feel that until you feel your trousers filling up with blood, or you feel warm wet

stuff trickling down your legs. I was sliced with a Stanley knife the first time I was stabbed. I knocked this fella out and walked away and I didn't realise he'd sliced me as I hit him. So that's very painful afterwards, but you don't actually feel it at all at the time, because it's such a sharp blade.

. That's not as dangerous as being plunged. Being plunged with a knife is very different from being sliced. For one thing, it hurts like fuck, straight away. I was once stabbed with a sharpened screwdriver on the door. But I was lucky – as the guy tried to get me, one of the other doormen was hanging round his neck and pulling him away, so I only got a partial plunge in the stomach area. I didn't get the full force of it. If that had gone all the way in and hit vital organs, I could easily have been dead.

If you actually get plunged with a screwdriver, it is more dangerous than a knife, because it's a blunt instrument and it goes in and does more tissue damage. That can be really serious.

Do women really need to build up muscle?
Yes. Most do, if they want to stay in shape. But 'muscle' is a dirty word for a lot of women. They think of big muscles, but if you hit the endurance cell in a muscle, the slow-twitch muscle fibre, you actually get lean, hard muscle. And muscle uses fat for energy, so that speeds up the metabolism. Muscle in a woman is often something that is sorely needed.

Men are lucky like that. They naturally have muscle density in their legs, because their endocrine systems are dominated by testosterone, rather than oestrogen. So men don't suffer from the dreaded cellulite – what my dictionary calls 'the herniation of subcutaneous fat in fibrous connective tissue, manifesting topographically as skin dimpling and nodularity'. Even if they weigh thirty stone and look like they're giving birth to triplets, men just don't get it.

When you mention building muscle, women are often worried that you're talking about bulging bodybuilder-type muscles. But there's a massive misconception here. If women don't build lean, hard muscle, they end up with slow metabolisms and when they're thirty-five or so they blow up and become the size of a house. We call them 'fat skinny birds' in the trade. When a fat skinny bird hits her mid-thirties, she will suddenly be four times the size, unless she eats like a rabbit. The way to keep that weight off is a fast metabolism, and a fast metabolism means lean, hard muscle.

Muscle makes you look good and feel better, too, as it pulls you in like a girdle and keeps everything tight. Women can lose inches and drop a dress size, and the faster metabolic rate means calories get burned and the weight will stay off. The changes we work on take a while, but you can see them start to show within weeks, with obviously significant improvements in about ninety days.

Have you still got any friends now from your teenage years?
I have. There's a lovely bloke called Trevor Schofield. Nothing to do with St Leonard's. He was a window dresser then, in a shop I worked in briefly, and we got to be good mates. He's done well for himself and become a big property developer. He owns half of Essex now, and a chunk of France, as well.

He's a good friend and he's been a very positive

influence on me – very hardworking and supportive. When we were kids, I used to go round to his house and his mum would always make a fuss of me.

'Paul, do you want some dinner with us?' she'd say.

And because Trevor always tells it like it is, they'd end up slipping into a little comedy routine.

'Of course he fucking does, mum. He's an orphan. He don't get fucking fed!'

'Trevor! Stop it! Why do you say things like that? He could be crying inside.'

'Oh fuck off, Mum. Just feed him.'

Trevor thought it was hilarious that his mum was so sensitive about my feelings, but the fact is, they were always just a really kind, generous family. You never know, at the time, when a big, important friendship is beginning, but Trevor's been there for me whenever I needed him, for nearly thirty-five years.

CHAPTER 22

EMOTIONAL INTELLIGENCE

There's a story I've known for years that has always stuck in my mind.

It's about twin boys, brought up in America by their brawling, boozing, scumbag father, after their mother died young. The father neglects the boys, hits them around and leaves them half-starved for days on end as he drinks and fights and steals. He's in and out of prison and the boys do well just to stay alive and survive it all. It's the childhood from hell, and it's bound to have a huge effect on them.

Years later, a journalist does an interview in a prison with some grubby, alcoholic down-and-out who's been picked up on a street corner and jailed for vagrancy. He asks him how his life came to be in this state. The guy explains that he was one of those twins.

'What do you expect, with a father like mine?' he says.

As a matter of interest, the journalist does what all good journos do and digs into the background to his story. He finds out where the other twin is living and goes to talk to him. It turns out he's a doctor, a specialist in alcohol-related diseases, and he's done very well for himself, with a nice house, a big car and a young family. The reporter asks how come he's got all this, when he came from such a terrible start in life, with no home to speak of and nothing going for him.

'What do you expect, with a father like mine?' he says.

It's corny as hell, of course. But I heard that story and it stuck with me.

Either you go along with what seems to be your fate, or you fight it. You need a bit of luck, now and again, and not everybody is going to make it. Accidents of birth come into it, of course, but most of what you become is up to you. I realised early on that while my poisoned childhood had damaged me in all sorts of ways, it wouldn't do me any good to spend the rest of my life blaming St Leonard's for everything that happened to me.

The tale of the two twins has been around for ages, though everyone tweaks the details in the retelling. A friend of mine traced it right back to a book by Dale Carnegie, the author of *How to Win Friends and Influence People*, and Carnegie died in 1955. The story probably goes back a lot further than that, though, because it sums up a real basic truth. Either you go with what you've got around you, or you kick against it. I chose to kick.

I've always been very interested in the idea of emotional intelligence (also known as EQ, or 'emotional quotient'). I think emotional intelligence is important – maybe the most important factor of the lot – in shaping many people's lives. I've certainly seen more than one person with a very impressive IQ come to grief because he didn't have the EQ to go with it.

My childhood mate, Liam, was the brightest kid in St Leonard's, without a doubt. When we moved up to secondary school, Liam was put in one of the top streams. And he stayed there, keeping up with the boys around him, despite never doing any homework. There was simply nowhere you could settle down to an hour's homework in St Leonard's. Neither the staff nor the other kids would have given you a moment's peace. But Liam kept going and kept on getting middling-good results.

I know now that Liam was really clever. He was a natural academic. If he'd had anything like a normal, supportive home background, he'd have been near the top of the top stream and he'd have sailed into university. To get middling-good results in the situation he was in was amazing. They should have given him a fucking PhD, just for beating the odds.

Liam's problem was emotional. From what I've been told by his family, I believe he'd been sexually molested at St Leonard's while he was still in nappies, by a person or persons unknown – and still, to this day, uninvestigated.

Liam was my best friend for ten years and I never knew. When I left St Leonard's and cut myself off completely from all the people – good and bad – who had had anything to do with my past, there were just two I regretted losing touch with. One was Liam, and the other one was Mary, the ex-nurse from the convent who had wanted to adopt me as a baby and who had taken me out on long day trips to the New Forest and holidays at the seaside throughout my childhood.

It's Mary's little white Mini I'm standing in front of with my bucket and spade in the old photo on the front of *Against All Odds*. We were on the beach at Southbourne, near Bournemouth, that day, and I was four.

I like that picture. It's the one and only photograph I have of me as a child.

Mary, of course, was – and still is – one of the most level-headed, well-adjusted, kind and forgiving creatures on this planet. She bubbles with emotional intelligence and curiosity about people. I still don't know what she felt when I broke off contact with her during my teenage turmoil, or what she really thought when I reappeared in her life, wanting to be friends again, after a break of twenty years. You just always have that feeling, with Mary, that everything's going to be OK.

Liam's life after St Leonard's was difficult, and short. As I said earlier, he died in 1999, committing suicide in front of a train. For the previous five years, he had been haunted by rape flashbacks.

As a child, Liam had always been strong, smart and funny. I'd looked up to him as my big brother, even though he was only a few months older than me. But I wasn't around to help when his life began to fall apart, in his late twenties. The police told me after his death that he had been 'schizophrenic', but I just think he was fucked. The damage that had been done to him was so deep below the skin that he didn't have that choice about whether to kick back against his destiny or not. His IQ was probably astronomical, if anyone had ever been bothered to measure it. But his emotional stability – an essential part of anyone's EQ – was shot to pieces.

I was lucky. I never had the wrenching, soul-searing experience of being raped, and my emotional core was battered, rather than shattered. Although I sustained heavy damage, it was largely repairable. Liam's damage was fatal.

When I look at my two boys now, I feel that helping them develop their emotional intelligence is a vital part of my role as their father. They need help to learn how to handle and react to other people and to their own feelings, and that's something I can provide.

Despite all the ups and downs of my life, I'm an optimist and I actually believe that most people are fundamentally good. Glass half full, I suppose. It's an attitude that is bound to rub off on them, and I hope it does. I think it helps kids, for example, to meet a lot of people and to spend time with adults in relaxed, informal situations.

Ever since Harley was crawling, I've brought him into my gym at home when I've had clients coming in. I've taught him, from a toddler, to say hello, look them in the eye and call them by their names. He's naturally easy around adults, and he's grown up seeing a lot of different people, listening to them and chatting with them and getting used to being in the company of strangers. Already he seems to me incredibly mature and relaxed for a nine-year-old, confident enough to enjoy acting on stage as a hobby, smart enough to shut up and learn from other people when the time is right.

We talk quite a lot about the people he meets and things that go on at school, and I'm always impressed at how level-headed my nine-year-old can be.

'Dad, why doesn't everyone like me?' he asked recently.

It's a good point. If I'm nice to people, why do some of

them still not like me? And I had to stop for a moment to find an answer. I wanted to tell him that some people are just arsy like that. With some people, no matter what you do, you won't get a positive reaction. I didn't want to dwell on it, but I wanted to make the point once, in some way that he'd remember, so it would be of use to him.

'Son,' I said, 'you can't polish a turd! Sometimes you just have to give up on people and move on.'

It's not elegant, but it's become one of Harley's favourite phrases. He's taken it to heart. When a jealous classmate started having a pop at him recently, he came back and discussed it with Jo and me. I pointed out that the other kid's behaviour was probably much more to do with how he felt about himself than anything to do with Harley. He should just let it go, unless it became a big problem.

'I did, Dad,' he said. 'I did let it go. He isn't worth polishing.'

Jo picked up on that straight away. I knew she would.

'Why did he say "polishing", Paul? What have you been teaching him?'

There was a moment's pause, then all three of us fell about laughing.

I knew that she knew that Harley knew that she knew what I'd said to him. And she knew that Harley knew that I'd said it like that because I wanted him to remember it for years to come. That's what happens when you marry a rough diamond like me – things get phrased in unusual and forthright ways. But I bet you Harley passes that little insight on to his own kids when the time comes. In fact, I've probably started a family tradition.

CHAPTER 23

HANDS

My family had its roots in Ireland, in Connemara, in a part of the world where the old folk traditions haven't all been brushed aside. The old people still hold onto all kinds of 'unscientific' beliefs – and the young people half-believe them, too. For my relatives in Connemara, the old idea that the seventh son of a seventh son is somehow special still means something.

According to tradition, a man like this is born lucky – and born with special powers. He can cure almost any wound or disease with the touch of his healing hands. And because my father was a seventh son, and I was his seventh boy, I am that man.

I don't know that I was necessarily born lucky. Being thrown out with the rubbish and suffering the gruesome experience of growing up among the sadists and paedophiles of the St Leonard's children's home is not everyone's idea of an enviable start in life.

But I do have a healing touch.

And there's nothing magical or mystical about it.

It's taken me nearly thirty years to learn what I know now about how bodies work and to develop the healing touch. It comes from a lot of studying in the first place, followed by many hours a week, year after year, working with real bodies, in the gym and on the massage table.

But that's a fantastic combination. In the gym, I get to help people lose weight, recover from injuries and operations and build up their strength, stamina and confidence. I see them change over the course of a few weeks. You see their appearance change as their bodies shape up, and you see unmistakable changes inside as well. Where there is a specific problem or we're doing rehab work after an injury, we see minor miracles of healing.

It's the body that heals itself, of course, but I know I can do a lot of hands-on work to help it succeed.

When it comes to massage, we're still at a strange in-between stage where people aren't really sure what it's for. If you call it physiotherapy, that sounds like real medicine. When you see rows of runners stretched out receiving massage after the London Marathon, that's clearly doing something useful. But people are very unclear about what massage might be able to do for them if they don't have a specific injury or strenuous sporting commitments. Apart from anything else, the way brothels are often set up as massage parlours helps confuse the picture.

Think of how the health system in Britain works. Your doctor is unable to spend a great deal of time getting to know the fine detail of your body and your problems. He or she may hardly physically touch you. But if I spend half an hour massaging your back or your leg, I will learn an enormous amount about what is going on.

Good massage involves taking in information all the time, through your hands. They can often tell you far more than the patient can put into words. The hands feel tensions and irregularities, distortions and uneven wear. The fingers can feel when muscles are knotted or hamstrings are tight. They are aware of sore or tender areas and they can tell you when movement is restricted or uncomfortable. Like a physiotherapist, the person carrying out the massage is engaging directly with the patient and his or her symptoms and reactions. In mainstream medicine, the only doctor who gets to know an individual patient's body that well is the surgeon. And while surgeons do a lot of homework beforehand, with their X-rays and MRI scans, the first time they touch the patient's body is usually with scalpel in hand. The feedback loops don't work too well, either, when someone's under anaesthetic.

I've studied a lot, over the years, exploring many different ways of conditioning and mending bodies. I've studied sports massage and anatomy, kinesthetics and kinesiology, nutrition and Pilates, Reiki and every type of exercise technique. But most of what you learn is really to do with instinct and experience. It's about learning to feel differences of density and muscle tone. You feel muscles and bones, tendons, ligaments and fascia, and you feel them all talk back to you. I don't always know where my hands are going next, but they go where they need to go, in response to the feedback that is coming through. It may be instinct, but it's instinct developed over maybe 15,000 hours of work like this. Like the guitarist's ability to play a solo without thinking or the footballer's spontaneous turn and shot, this is instinct and training and experience coming together faster than conscious thought will allow.

I love rehabilitation work and I've done a hell of a lot of it now, with great results. Apart from all the usual sports injuries, I've helped people with multiple sclerosis become stronger and more mobile and I've also had good results with those whose lives are blighted by ME or chronic fatigue syndrome. But one of the areas that interests me most at the moment is working with young people suffering from scoliosis, or curvature of the spine. This can be anything from a slight bending to a severe, sharp S-curve, but even in its milder forms it is often ugly, painful and restrictive. Scoliosis often strikes hard during a kid's adolescent growth spurt and it seems to affect more girls than boys.

Braces and corsets are usually tried first, but they are uncomfortable and often don't work. Kids hate them. Eventually, the options may narrow down to surgery, which is a big thing for a young person, involving operations lasting four hours or more, with permanent fusion of part of the spine and sometimes the insertion of rods, wires, hooks and screws. You wouldn't wish that on anyone, if it could be avoided.

I have worked with scoliosis patients for several years now, and I've been delighted to discover that my combination of massage and gym-based muscle conditioning can produce some fantastic results. Word gets around and I've now got people queuing up to come and see me. I've been working with several girls recently who were already scheduled to have major back surgery for scoliosis and have shown such obvious improvements that these operations have been cancelled.

I'd better say here that claiming to be able to improve or cure scoliosis through massage and conditioning is controversial. The Scoliosis Association (UK), for example, takes a pessimistic view of what it calls 'complementary therapies'. Though it does not specifically mention massage, its website does dismiss physiotherapy and related approaches as ineffective:

'There is no reliable evidence that techniques such as osteopathy, chiropractic, physiotherapy, reflexology, or acupuncture can make any difference to a potentially increasing spinal curvature. If patients are told that an established spinal curvature can be cured by any of these techniques, they should not accept that information as true. Only surgery, and sometimes bracing, can substantially affect the curvature.'

There's no way I can prove how wrong that is. It's absolute cobblers. It's infuriating. I can't commission large-scale double-blind trials to provide conclusive statistical evidence. All I can do is point to a string of patients and their parents who are relieved and delighted at the improvements we have created between us – and to the list of cancelled NHS operations.

I've just been working with a long-term client, Evie, a twenty-two-year-old I've helped with scoliosis. She's been having stomach pains for months and was recently in hospital for nine days for tests to try and figure out what's wrong. The base of Evie's spine curves to the left and this has led to weak and undeveloped muscles on the right-hand side. The big vertical erector spinae muscles either side of her backbone are much weaker on the right. This was forcing the hip muscles to do too much, causing the groin strain that has made the hip flexors tighten up and pull on the abdomen, causing her pain. As I worked away to loosen up her back muscles, the chain of cause and effect was broken and the pain was reduced almost immediately. Anyone who'd touched those bunched and knotted abdominal muscles would have been able to feel what was wrong. But doctors don't touch. It was a musculo-skeletal problem and no one had noticed. Evie had been tested for everything from irritable bowel syndrome and kidney stones to ectopic pregnancy, and all that time, effort and public money had just been wasted.

This is not the place for a full explanation of how I successfully treat scoliosis. But it's important to say that I don't try to move the patient's spine. This is all soft tissue work and I'm not trying to change the skeleton at all. I don't need to. I use sports massage techniques to gradually work out the angry knots and spasms in overworked muscles, with a lot of work over quite a long period of time, and I use specialist conditioning work to make non-working muscles fire and develop strength and start doing their job again. Once the muscles are in balance and working properly, the soft tissue itself provides support and holds everything in position.

What we're doing has nothing to do with miracles. These programmes take a lot of hard work. The patient has to be ready to put up with ninety-minute sessions of hard conditioning work in the gym and painful deep tissue massage twice a week for at least a couple of months, plus home workouts five days a week.

It's not easy, but it's worth it. Grace, one twelve-year-old girl I've been working with, was in tears in the doctor's surgery two months ago when she was told she'd need to have a major op this summer. Her mother brought her to me on the recommendation of another client of mine. Now she's had thirteen sessions and she's out of pain and out of her back brace, and the appointment for surgery has been cancelled.

There's still quite a lot of work to do, to build up the muscles so they are symmetrical and balanced and support her spine properly. We'll need to work out a follow-up exercise programme, a maintenance programme, but it will be much less intense now. Grace's mother, Claire Harman, sent me before-and-after photographs, so that I could put them up on my website, alongside her own comment on her daughter's progress.

'She feels so much better – and no big horrible operation for her,' she wrote on Facebook. 'Not only is he helping her scoliosis, he has helped build her confidence and her general health has lifted. He's made a big difference to her life.

'We still have a long way to go, building up her underworked muscles, but the difference in her back and posture already is amazing. And she no longer spends her days in that awful back brace.'

Another back sufferer, who had been in pain for eight years after injury at work, wrote me an email the other day to say that he was now pain-free. He'd seen any number of specialists and had practically resigned himself to living with the problem for ever.

'Now I am getting my quality of life back,' he said. 'Thank you, Paul, from the bottom of my heart.'

Just reading comments like those makes me proud of what I've learned and what I've become. Like getting *Against All Odds* written and published and telling the world about the children of St Leonard's, being able to help people like this makes me feel I really have left the horrible curse of Auntie Coral far behind me.

Recently there have been some flattering bits of recognition that have come to me from various directions. I was named 'Essex Businessman of the Year' and there's a Pinterest site dedicated to Inspirational Men, where I'm listed alongside Steven Spielberg, Nelson Mandela and Gok Wan. Now do you understand why I've never been quite sure where I fit in?

I'm not perfect, but I'm not the useless, doomed piece of shit Coral always told me I would be. I've never been to prison. I learned to read and write, eventually – not well, and not easily, but enough. I've built a family, a home and a business, and I have discovered how to combine making a living with making people's lives better.

I am able to use my early experiences to help important causes like Sue Porto's literacy work with Beanstalk, to give the boys at the Ramsden Hall school a bit of help in sorting themselves out, and to add a different perspective to Lord Listowel's campaigns to professionalise the care industry and provide a better start for children coming out of care.

I always thought my hands would be the key to my future. I thought I'd be using them to box my way to the top, or at least to a well-paid career. So it was a cruel irony that the fall that nearly killed me permanently damaged my right hand – and, of course, needless to say, I am right-handed. I suppose it's ironic all over again that a major part of my work now is one of the most hands-on jobs you can imagine.

It's hard to sum up what I've learned. Except that it turns out many problems that are usually tackled with drugs or surgery can be treated as well or better with the combination of massage and conditioning. Many doctors simply don't know what can be done. Our bodies can do so much to put themselves right, if you do the right things to help them. And I've also learned that there is much more connection than is often assumed between people's moods and confidence and their physical state. That traffic goes in both directions. Helping someone improve their fitness, strength and stamina or removing distracting pain can change their lives by making them feel better about themselves and stopping them from doubting their potential.

More broadly, I've learnt that families work, if you really work at them. That's something I didn't believe for most of my life. I thought people who talked about their wonderful childhood and marvellous family life were either kidding themselves or trying to kid me. After all those years when I could never imagine being a devoted husband and a dedicated father, I still haven't got over my surprise at finding I can do it, and make a good job of it, too.

I even do the soppy stuff well. We have a routine we go through when I put the boys to bed at night, and there's always the same conversation with Archie, who's four now.

'What are we going to dream about tonight, then, Arch?' I ask him.

And he snuggles down under his duvet and tells me which of his favourite things the night's entertainment will feature – dogs or snowmen, friends from school or Thomas the Tank Engine, Santa or rainbows – before drifting off into his little world.

Above all, I've learnt that trying to tough life out, doing other people down and blaming it all on what you've been through is no way to live. I came through a nightmare childhood – not quite as bad as those of the worst victims of St Leonard's, but bad enough to leave some deep and lasting wounds – and somehow survived to come out the other side.

I've made it, more or less in one piece, beating the odds that were stacked against me when I was dumped by my parents, abused by my carers, let down by the system and left, battered and illiterate, to find my own way in the world. Now I've learned that I can use my background and experiences to help and inspire others – and that it's really important that I should do that.

They say nothing's ever wasted. That only applies if you find ways to make good use of it. I've come a long way, but there's still a long way to go.

ABANDONED AS A BABY, I WAS ONE OF FEW
SURVIVORS OF THE MOST BRUTAL CARE SYSTEM.
THIS IS THE STORY OF HOW I FOUGHT BACK.

AGAINST ALL ODDS

PAUL CONNOLLY

THE MOST AMAZING TRUE-LIFE
STORY YOU'LL EVER READ

The free first chapter of Paul Connolly's bestselling
Against All Odds - The Most Amazing True Life Story
You'll Ever Read...

CHAPTER 1

GROWING UP BAD

It had been many years since I had seen any of the children who had grown up with me, who had been my sisters and brothers throughout my childhood and adolescence. When I left the children's home at St Leonard's, I promised myself that I would have nothing to do with them ever again; that the past was over and the future, such as it was, was in my own hands. I was sure that my only chance of living a good life would be to put the past behind me, even though that meant saying goodbye to some of the people I loved the most – as well as the ones I hated more than words could even begin to express.

For people in my world, it was never good news when the police knocked on the door, and I had several good reasons to be anxious on this particular occasion. I knew them as soon as they turned up; police have a distinctive way of knocking that one becomes familiar with over the years. I peered out of the window at them to confirm my suspicions, but I didn't answer the door, hoping that they would just give up and go away quietly. I didn't think I had anything to answer for at present, in any case. I was used to avoiding contact with the police, usually with good reason.

They kept coming back, two female constables in plain clothes that did nothing to conceal the fact that they were police officers. Eventually, I decided that, if the police were really going to nick me, they would not have sent two women. The police knew me well and they knew that I would easily be able to take out two men, let alone a couple of girls, if I were so inclined.

I answered the door. I didn't open it all the way; I did not want to look too welcoming.

'What's up?'

The women looked at me with a degree of sympathy. One of them smiled. She was a real stunner; a gorgeous young woman whose formal, tailored clothing did nothing to hide her shapely body. I relaxed a little. I may have even smiled.

'Can we come in for a moment?'

'I suppose.'

I stood aside and the two women walked in the door of the first home I had ever owned and paid for on my own.

'You might want to sit down,' one of them advised me. 'We've got bad news, and you should prepare yourself for a shock.'

'I'm fine.'

I stayed standing. I don't like people telling me what to do, especially in my own home, even if they are pretty young women.

'It's about St Leonard's.'

'St Leonard's? What about it?'

St Leonard's was the children's home where I had grown up, in the part of East London that spills over into Essex. I had not been inside its doors for years, and I did my best to think about it as little as possible. Years before, I had decided that I was fucked up enough on my own; I didn't need to have to deal with the stress of being around or even thinking about other fucked-up people. Quite the reverse – I needed to seek out the company of sane, normal people and focus as hard as I could on keeping things together for myself. That was the only way to sort my life out. I had cut all my ties with my past, my family and the children's home where I had spent the worst years of my life. If you lie in shit, you smell of shit.

I didn't want to smell of shit.

'What is it?' I asked the police officer. 'I haven't been to St Leonard's for donkey's years. What's all this got to do with me?'

'Paul, it has been brought to our attention that, of the eight children in your dorm, only two of you are still alive.' She paused. The two women looked at me solicitously.

I sat down. I was only thirty-five. Surely that wasn't right. How could all those boys with whom I had grown up be dead? It didn't make sense. I waited for her explanation. It turned out that six of us had died, several by slow suicide in the form of heroin abuse, and at least two by faster means.

'There have been complaints made of serious abuse, including sexual abuse, during the period when you were at St Leonard's. A major investigation is ongoing, and we would like to talk to you. We are going to have to talk to everyone who grew up in St Leonard's when you were there, but your name in particular has come up in some of the evidence we have been hearing. Apparently, you were a witness to the attempted rape of one of the other children...'

'Tell me what happened to the other boys,' I requested numbly.

The policewoman listed the names of the boys who had been like my brothers when I was growing up. One of my old friends, Mark Byrnes, had taken a dive into oblivion off Beachy Head. You've got to be more than a little desperate to do something like that. Liam, who had been my very best friend throughout all the years of my childhood, had jumped on the tracks at Mile End Station and died under the wheels of a commuter train. What could be worse than that? What had happened to him that had made him so desperate? I wasn't even sure that I wanted to know.

'He was schizophrenic, apparently,' the woman said of Liam's death, as if that was a mitigating factor. As if that made it less awful.

Liam was dead. Liam. I felt sick. I wanted to hold my head in my hands and close my eyes but I just sat and stared at her as she continued: 'We've started an investigation into the St Leonard's children's home, Operation Mapperton, to find out what went on there and why so few of you are still alive. We understand that you grew up in Wallis Cottage which was –' she checked her paperwork '– run by William Starling.'

Starling. I had not heard that name for years. In an instant, I was reduced to the little boy who had been told every day,

'You're rubbish. You'll never amount to anything. Look at you, you fucking retard. You Irish lowlife scum. You're just a bloody Connolly, aren't you? Prison fodder from the day you were born, you little shit. Who ever loved you? Nobody, that's who... and nobody ever fucking will.'

My parents were Irish, from the beautiful wilds of Connemara, on the windy Atlantic seaboard, on the most westerly coast of the European continental shelf. My father was the seventh son in a family of fourteen, and my mother, a trained midwife, was from a smaller family, also local. My father, Matthew, had grown up in a minuscule labourer's cottage in the middle of nowhere in rural Galway, and had a lot of poverty to escape from. My mother, Mary, was from rather more affluent circumstances; her father owned a local pub, which meant that he was one of the wealthier people in the area. I don't think he was very impressed when his daughter married a boy from a rough cottage. My parents had already had six children together when, like so many Irish people in the late fifties and early sixties, they came to look for work in the East End of London. Now, Connemara is one of Ireland's most loved tourist destinations, but back then it was a poor place, the rough stony ground challenging the local farmers to eke out a meagre living, and jobs and a good livelihood painfully difficult to come by.

The idea seems to have been that my father would make a living in the building trade in London, like so many Irishmen before him, and presumably my mother thought that she might pick up work as a midwife. In those days Irish healthcare workers were very highly trained and, every year, thousands of London babies were delivered by Irish midwives. The money they sent back to Ireland when they emigrated helped to prop up the crippled economy of what was still a very backward island.

At that point, everything seems to have started falling irreparably apart for my parents and for all their children. I don't know the details, but apparently my mother kicked my father out before I was even born, perhaps because she was seeing another man. I have never known either of my parents, but the impression I have gained was that my mum was an attractive woman with no shortage of attention from men.

When I was two weeks old, my mother left me out beside the rubbish bins near her home in Stepney Green. I was a small baby with jet-black hair. One of the neighbours heard my cries and took me in and called Social Services, who came and collected me and handed me into the care of the nuns of St Vincent's in Mill Hill, which was in Hendon in North London. I was the seventh son of a seventh son, but it did not bring me a lot of luck back then.

From the moment my mother dumped me on the side of the street with the rubbish, I would see her only a handful of times in the course of my childhood. I never knew her.

Together with scores of other babies, I would stay in St Vincent's nursery until I was four or five, and then move into a big dormitory with the other children. Although a great deal of this phase of my life is, of course, quite hazy, I have some memories from the period, and especially of our favourite game, which was to leave the dormitory by means of the window and then leap precariously from one window ledge to another, high above the ground. That must have been when I lost the first of my nine lives, because, if we had fallen, we would have been goners, that's for sure.

I also remember that, every so often, one of the children from St Vincent's nursery was adopted and taken away by new parents. For the rest of the children, this was amazing. One day our little friend would be there eating and getting dressed and undressed and going to bed with the rest of us, and the next he would be gone and we would be told that he had been taken away to live with a 'mum' and a 'dad'. The very concept of a nuclear family was not familiar to us, and the whole business seemed to be wrapped in a cloak of mystery.

As a healthy, white male who had been given up as a newborn, I should have been a prime candidate for would-be adoptive parents. In fact, one of the nurses at the home, Mary Littler, was very fond of me and tried to adopt me, even though she was still a very young woman at the time, about twenty years old. My mother put paid to that. Biological parents could veto any adoption of their children by displaying some meagre interest in their welfare, and I believe that my mother came to visit me about once a year, although I don't remember those visits and don't know why she was so resistant to having me adopted, as she clearly had no interest in me herself. Mary also told me that my father, who was then working nights, came to visit me every day when I was very small.

I have often wondered how my life would have turned out if I had become Mary's adopted son; if someone had loved me as a child, as I love my little boys today.

I am still in touch with Mary, who lives on the south coast now. She has provided me with some of the sparse information I have about my origins. Mary told me that my father had done his best to keep the family together after my parents separated, and that he had even got back with my mother at one stage so as to get all of us kids out of care, but that once again our mother had ensured that we would stay just where we were. After a while, my father drifted away, too. From that moment, both my parents became strangers to me and they have remained so ever since.

One of my earliest memories is that of reaching the age of three or four and suddenly realising in a moment of clarity that I was utterly alone in the world. Every child growing up in care has that realisation at an early age. All of a sudden, with awful, shocking clarity of vision, you know that you are all alone and that, ultimately, nobody even cares whether you live or die because the world is indifferent to the children who nobody loves. Nobody wants you. Nobody ever wanted you. It is the loneliest feeling in the world. It is utterly overwhelming. I have been through it myself and I have seen it happen, again and again, to the younger children in the home where I grew up. I think that, when this terrible realisation happened to me, I changed overnight from being quite a friendly, outgoing child to a difficult, shy child with a tendency to lash out that I have never managed to get completely under control. That dreadful under-standing, of being utterly alone and unloved, shatters confidence and hope the way nothing else can.

Just before I turned eight, I was taken from the only home I had ever known and brought by my social worker Mr Gardner, an elegantly dressed black man, to St

Leonard's Home for Children in Essex, on the outskirts of East London. The home was a complex of beautiful Victorian buildings that had been created in what was then the green Essex countryside, to provide London's unwanted offspring with a healthy country childhood that would give them a great foundation in life. By the time that I was sent to live there, in the late 1960s, London had grown so much that it had engulfed the countryside and the home, which was now run by Tower Hamlets. I had been told that I had a brother there, but we had not had any contact, so I did not know Declan any more than any of the other children I was about to meet. I knew that I had six brothers and one sister and I had met the ones closest to me in age, but I had little understanding of what being related meant. We had all been rejected by our mother, but the older ones had spent a large portion of their childhoods at home.

I am the youngest, after John. Then come Danny, Declan, Peter, Matthew, Michael and Anne. At least our mother had been consistent in not having any interest in any of her children. Several of my siblings had done time in St Vincent's, and Matty and Michael, who were much older, were in a more secure unit in Bedfordshire. We had nothing to do with each other then; we have almost nothing to do with each other now. I do talk to Matty once in a while on the phone, but we don't actually meet much. Blood is not really thicker than water; if you don't grow up with your sisters and brothers, they are not really family.

Back then, as I was brought to St Leonard's children's home, I wondered if Declan and I would get to know each other better. I was led by the hand down the long, winding avenue to the cottage I would share with about thirty other children and our house parent, Bill Starling, a man who was then in his mid–forties, having been at the home for about two years. I was told that we children were supposed to refer to him as 'Uncle Bill'. Some of the other care workers there were also referred to as 'Aunties' and there was one in particular who I had the misfortune of having as one of my carers. I can't tell you her real name for legal reasons but I'll refer to her simply as 'Auntie Coral'.

When I met up with Declan, he gave me some inside information. Until recently, the housemother who had been taking care of him had been a kind, older woman called Peggy, whom the children referred to affectionately as 'wooden tit' because of the prosthetic breast she wore following an operation for breast cancer. I do not know how Peggy felt about her nickname, but it did seem to be meant well. The children had all liked Peggy and she seemed to have provided them with a degree of security and some sense of being cared for. Unfortunately for me, Peggy had by now retired.

Starling was still quite new, and apparently Declan had not quite got the measure of him yet, or else did not want to talk about it for some reason. The Principal of the home was a man called Alan Prescott, and I was strongly advised by Declan and all the other kids I met to keep out of his way, for reasons that would soon become very clear.

At St Leonard's, there were fourteen 'cottages', each of which housed up to thirty kids. At the home, we had our own orchards, playground, sick bay, swimming pool and gardens. It all looked beautiful and someone had clearly put a lot of thought into building a wonderful environment for

London's unwanted kids. We were there for all sorts of reasons, although I was in a minority, having been unceremoniously dumped by my mother as a babe-in-arms. We had rent boys who had been 'saved' from the streets as teenagers, riddled with sexually transmitted diseases and serious behaviour problems; children whose parents had voluntarily given them up for one reason or another; and children who had been taken from their parents by the social workers for the usual reasons of neglect, indifference and abuse. Occasionally, a child would come and stay at St Leonard's for a short period while his or her case was being decided, but the vast majority of us were there for the duration of our childhood and teenage years and, for us, St Leonard's was the only home that we knew.

We were all different, but we had one thing in common: we were all miserably, desperately unhappy. Not a lot of thought had gone into selecting the house parents who served at St Leonard's – or perhaps it had, albeit not in the way one would expect, and we certainly were not receiving anything even vaguely resembling proper childcare.

Before deciding to go into the care industry, Bill Starling had been a lorry driver. In those days, astonishing as it seems, there was no vetting system for house parents, and he had no particular experience in caring for children. For Uncle Bill, the job at St Leonard's was a way to skim the system, pocket the proceeds and brutalise the kids in the process. Most of us were very small and thin for our age, and the reason why was simple – we were fed on bread and margarine and not much else, while Starling used the housekeeping budget for himself.

On my very first night – remember that I was just eight

years old and that I had just left the only home that I had never known – I wet the bed. Of course, I was desperately embarrassed. But, as if that was not bad enough, Auntie Coral made me strip off my sheets and then threw me and the sheets together into a bath of freezing cold water heavily laced with bleach where she scrubbed me until I was almost bleeding. This was the standard approach at St Leonard's to children with bedwetting problems. Unsurprisingly, Auntie Coral's attempts to cure us of bedwetting were less than effective. Most of the little ones wet their beds frequently, and the same treatment was always doled out.

I soon learned what happened when we children misbehaved in any way. Several times a week, we would be rooted out of our dorms and told to strip off all of our identical white-and-grey striped pyjamas – which resembled nothing more than the prison garb of caricature prisoners in old comic books – and line up in the hallway, while Starling, sometimes with some of his friends, walked up and down shouting, kicking our legs out from under us and stubbing out their cigarettes on our pigeon-chested bodies. They found this funny. They found it hilarious. Uncle Bill always had a cigarette in his hand. He was a chain smoker who lit up and puffed away in front of the children, regardless of what was going on. This also meant that he always had a handy tool at the ready to inflict pain on our tender skin.

When the adults had tired of the entertainment, we would be allowed to put on our nightclothes and leave. I do remember that this sort of thing would happen more often in the summertime. We would all be sent to bed at the usual early time but, because it was summer, it was still light, and none of us could sleep, so we would start messing about, tossing pillows and generally acting up. Then Bill Starling would come roaring up to the dormitory and root us out, yelling, 'Get out into the hall, you little bastards! Get the fuck out of bed, you little shits,' and the entertainment would begin, especially on those evenings when he had friends over and they had all been drinking. While Uncle Bill was not a particularly heavy drinker, a beer or two seemed to help him to shed whatever few inhibitions he still had. Uncle Bill liked to show his friends that the kids he was in charge of knew who the boss was, and he was single-minded in pursuit of this goal.

Apart from Uncle Bill's incursions into the dormitory, there was little at St Leonard's to break the monotony of everyday life. In the morning, we got up at around seven, got our breakfast and went to school. In the evening, we came home, ate, watched TV for a while and went to bed. We were periodically instructed to wash, and generally made to take care of ourselves in terms of personal hygiene. Nothing ever really changed, and every day was pretty much the same as the one that went before it in one long, depressing litany. Birthdays were not celebrated – which was at least honest, because we all knew that nobody was very happy about the fact that we unwanted rascals had been born. In fact, mine was usually marked in the form of birthday greetings on the second of August – when I had actually been born on the twenty-second. In a good year, a local factory would donate toys at Christmas, which we would all share, because there was little question of any child having personal possessions, which would have led inevitably to jealousy and squabbling. Christmas dinner stands out, as Christmas Day was the only day in the year when we would eat well. Some of the children would have gone home to see relatives for the holidays, so there would be less of us about, and we would have a proper roast turkey and other good things and stuff ourselves until we felt sick, and then watch the better-than-usual fare on television.

The kids of St Leonard's were a motley crew of mostly Irish and black boys and girls. They were the offspring of already dysfunctional families, like the Connollys, who had come to London with the idea that they would get ahead and prosper, only to find that the streets were not paved with gold after all. Their old problems were still with them and now there was no support system to hold everything together as there might have been at home. In those days, the perception was that the most dysfunctional people in Britain were usually either Irish or black, which is why, if you look at old newsreels, you'll see the signs landlords used to post in their windows: 'No blacks, Irish or dogs'. Irish and black petty criminals flooded borstals and prisons, and most of the drunks cooling off in the police cells were from the same demographic. Even at the young age of the children in the home, we were seen as the lowest form of life there was, and treated accordingly.

It was not fair, but people who come from the toughest, hardest, most poverty-stricken backgrounds are often going to be the most difficult to deal with and the most likely to become dangerous, truculent people, and the most likely to get drunk and make a nuisance of themselves. I saw this for myself, growing up, and later when I visited a relative in borstal where he was serving time for mugging old ladies. In his lock-up, as elsewhere, the prisoners were mostly Irish or black – there were no white, English grammar-school boys there!

At the home, we children often got into fights, but we were also like sisters and brothers and, perhaps surprisingly, we were colour-blind. Nobody cared who was Irish and who was black because we had so much in common; we were all abandoned runts who had been thrown on the tender – or not so tender – mercy of the state. We would fight over the last scrap of bread on the table or what we watched on television, but we didn't care what colour anyone was or where their parents had come from.

My best friend at St Leonard's was a little boy called Liam Carroll – another Irish child – who was in much the same boat as me. Liam lived in the cottage directly opposite mine, Myrtle Cottage. The windows of our cottages faced each other and, when we had to return to our respective buildings, Liam and I would part reluctantly. We would go to our dormitories and wave at each other through the windows, a strangely comforting ritual. I can still remember seeing his pale face through the slightly warped old glass, as though I was looking at him underwater. I didn't know how Liam had ended up in the home. He had a bigger brother but I never learned how they had been abandoned and this was not something we ever discussed. I imagine that it was another sad little tale of dysfunction and lack of love.

Liam and I were inseparable for years. To this day, I have to say that he was one of the strongest people I have ever known. It seemed to me then that, no matter what life threw at him, Liam would be OK. Even as a child, Liam appeared to be a pillar of strength. The only really happy memories I have from my childhood involve Liam. We bunked off school together whenever possible, and made our way to a nearby field where horses bound for the abattoir were kept. We enlivened the final days of those unhappy horses by jumping on them and riding bareback until we fell off. When we did go to school, we would walk the five miles there so as to save our bus fare to spend on sweets and other cheap carbohydrates that made us feel briefly full.

On one occasion, all the kids from the home had been taken over to Holland to do a hundred-mile march from Nijmegen to Arnhem, together with a bunch of boy scouts in uniform. Finding ourselves in the local red-light district, Liam and I spent so long eyeballing the girls that we missed our lift back to the youth hostel in the depths of the forest, and had to make our own way back in the dark, getting there just before the search parties were sent out.

These might not sound like typically happy boyhood memories, but they are what I have and they make me smile. For me, Liam was a real big brother, and I think he loved me, too.